THE POOR NUT

A COMEDY IN THREE ACTS

BY

J. C. NUGENT AND ELLIOTT NUGENT

Preface by Don Marquis

COPYRIGHT, 1925, BY SAMUEL FRENCH

All Rights Reserved

NEW YORK	LONDON
SAMUEL FRENCH	SAMUEL FRENCH, LTD.
PUBLISHER	26 SOUTHAMPTON STREET
25 WEST 45TH STREET	STRAND, W.C.2

THE POOR NUT

All Rights Reserved

The following is a copy of program of the first perform-
ance of "THE POOR NUT," as produced at the Henry
Miller Theatre, New York, N. Y., week beginning Monday evening, April 27, 1925:

PATTERSON McNUTT
Presents
"THE POOR NUT"
A Comedy of Modern Youth
By J. C. Nugent and Elliott Nugent
(Authors of "KEMPY")
with
ELLIOTT NUGENT
Staged by Howard Lindsay

CHARACTERS
(In order of their first appearance)

"Colonel" Small	*Joseph Dailey*
Margerie Blake	*Norma Lee*
John Miller	*Elliott Nugent*
Julia Winters	*Florence Shirley*
"Spike" Hoyt	*Grant Mills*
"Hub" Smith	*Beach Cooke*
"Magpie" Welch	*Percy Helton*
Coach Jackson	*John Webster*
"Wallie" Pierce	*Cornelius Keefe*
Professor Deming	*Wright Kramer*
"Doc" Spurney	*Thomas Shearer*
A Freshman	*Joseph Mitchell*
Wisconsin Official	*Robert Scott*
Reggie	*Margaret Fitch*
Betty	*Jean Mann*
Doris	*Frances Bavier*

Ohio State Students, Wisconsin Students

Runners

Wisconsin—Gavin O'Rourke, Frank Subers, Hamilton
Ward.
Ohio—Roger Briner, Lester Nielsen.

Act I. *The University Book Store.*
Act II. Scene I—*The Trainer's Tent, Athletic Field*
(*Next day*).
Scene II—*Official Boxers, corner of the Sta-
dium.*
Act III. *Living Room "Psi Sigma" House.* (*That
night*).

CAST
(See note below)

COLONEL SMALL, *Proprietor of the University Book-store*

MARJORIE BLAKE, *a college girl.*

JULIA WINTERS, *a Wisconsin co-ed*

JOHN MILLER, *"our hero"*

"HUB" SMITH, *a student*

"MAGPIE" WELCH, *the cheer-leader*

"SPIKE" HOYT, *Captain of Wisconsin track team*

WALLIE PIERCE, *Captain of Ohio State track team*

PROFESSOR DEMING, *of the Botany Department*

COACH JACKSON, *the track coach*

DOC SPURNEY, *the trainer*

THE OFFICIAL STARTER *(See note)*

A FRESHMAN, *a gawky kid of seventeen or eighteen*

BETTY ⎫
REGGIE ⎬ *Girls at the dance, Act III*
HELEN ⎭

TWO OHIO RUNNERS ⎫
THREE WISCONSIN RUNNERS ⎬ *In the race, Act II*

A CROWD OF "ROOTERS" *(At least thirty should be used)*

OFFICIAL ANNOUNCER *(Offstage. Done by "Official Starter")*

(NOTE: "Ed Small" can easily double the "Official Start-er." If short of men it is possible for him to double "Doc Spurney." Letting Doc Spurney act as official starter in the race scene will cut out the small part of the Starter, but is not recommended unless necessary, as it is usual for such officials in athletic meets to be from some neutral college. The two small parts of "Betty" and "Reggie" in Act III can be blended very easily if desired. The crowd of supers can be re-cruited from local amateurs and schools at very little expense and can learn the songs, cheers and business of the race scene very well in two rehearsals.)

SYNOPSIS OF SCENES

ACT I: *The University bookstore. June.*

ACT II. SCENE I: *The trainer's tent, Athletic Field.
Next day.*
SCENE II: *The track in front of a corner
of the stadium. Five minutes later.*

ACT III: *Living room, Psi Sigma House. That
night.*

IMPORTANT

(Note for "John Miller" and "Director")

The part of John Miller must not be overplayed for
comedy. Go after the heart interest of this character
and the comedy will play itself. If this part is
"hoked" it spoils the play.

PREFACE

"The Poor Nut," and the general type of play of which it is representative, belong to a class of art which could never have been produced in any country and any era but the America of here and now. I insist on the word Art, and I make the statement deliberately and sweepingly, in the hope of arousing the anger of whatever high-brow may read. The play is spirited, amusing, jolly, wholesome, and it has a happy ending. And how a certain type of high-brow critic and his followers loathe the word wholesome! How they hate and contemn the happy ending! They believe and they preach that nothing that is wholesome or happy can possibly be Art; nothing that is happy or wholesome can possibly have any relation to Life.

For they have been instructed about Art and Life by the European masters, and they are so essentially provincial that they insist that the American craftsman must imitate the European masters; he must always find Life as discouraging as the most melancholy Scandinavian or Russian of them all, or he is not real, he is not honest—he is not Significant. (Significant and Important are the great words!) Anything joyous must be untrue and trivial, any episode that is triumphant and unclouded must falsify existence; there must be defeat somewhere, there must be the sense of shadow encroaching upon

5

even the lighter moods and moments, there must be at least the apprehension of failure or unfulfillment in affairs spiritual or material,—or else a lie has been uttered in the teeth of the Cosmos and an insult has been offered to the Norns. Even in comedy, we must feel Urth, Verthandi, and Skuld in the background, looking askance at human endeavorings for a space of light-hearted happiness, and smiling cynically at the human hope that there has been or is or can be anything continuingly fortunate and victorious in the past, present or future of any individual. Such is the creed of the unintelligent bone-heads who refer to each other as the *intelligencia*.

They are wrong, and they are stupidly wrong. The European masters are honest—they have represented the life about them truly, they have been faithful to its letter and its spirit; I do not doubt it; and what they have seen and felt and responded to these many decades has been, when it has been more than superficial, predominently hopeless. For the common man of Europe, millions and millions of him, has been in a devil of a mess in one way or another for scores of years, for centuries. The immigrants who come hither will truly tell us as much, even if we do not read the literature of the masters.

The discovery of many honest American writers of the past century is that life is not hopeless in America for the common man. I know that there are thousands, hundreds of thousands, even millions, in America affected by poverty, and disease, and social and industrial injustice, and victimized by many oppressions, and denied the fulfilment of the promises made by the optimistic founders of the republic—but I also know, and you know too, if you are honest about it, that here and now in America for the great majorities of the ordinary inhabitants there really does exist the fuel and food for such hopefulness as nowhere exists in Europe, and there exists a spirit of hopefulness generally that is not found there. In short, the blither and more victorious outlook upon life and its problems spiritual and material which has been adopted by certain of our popular American writers is justified by the life which they find about them.

The false thing, the inartistic thing, the unreal thing, would be to suppress the utterances of this more optimistic mood in American life. The outlook upon heaven and earth on this continent is different, and the artist who fails to respond to such differences is not honest. I am not saying that life in America does not have its sordidness, its tragedies of disillusionment, its ghastly frustrations, its terrors for the sensitive and discerning soul, its problems of maladjustment and wickedness, its martyrdoms and tyrannies and crucifixions, its failures and despairs and futilities and perversions, its grotesqueries and ironies, its acrid comedies, its lacerating stupidities, its lies and defeats, its humours too bitter for either tears or laughter. But I do say that there exist, besides all this, great wide stretches of life played upon and suffused with a cheerful native sunlight of hopefulness and success; and that these stretches also are legitimate settings for stories and dramas that need not be untrue because they are not unhappy.

The contribution of this play is that it shows several millions of American young men and women, from Maine to Oregon, at a glance, living joyously and youthfully in the midst of this fortunate environment and breathing and floating in this atmosphere, and shows them truly, and with an understanding that is both penetrating and genial. It is not uncritical of their obvious faults, but it does not falsify their essential spirit. The particular problems of the hero are in themselves a criticism of the life in which he finds himself; it would have been possible to predicate the same set of facts and turn the story into a soul's tragedy—but it would have been no truer to the things that are. Personally, I like it better for not ending with a vista of wreck and ruin, or having anywhere in it the suggestion of the corpse of an illegitimate baby carried out in the ash-can.

DON MARQUIS.

THE POOR NUT

ACT I

SCENE: *The interior of the University Bookstore in Columbus, Ohio. A somewhat shallow set, with high shelves of books at the back and down the right side. Sections labelled "English," "French," "Spanish," "Italian," "Chemistry," "Mathematics," "Philosophy," "Psychology," etc.*

In the left upper corner a door (door should have large pane of glass—practical—covered with coating of Bon Ami for cleaning business. No real glass needed in window which should be a show window with space for display). Outside of door is a vestibule backing, and below the door a large window, with the letters "University Bookstore" painted on the outside, reversed within. This window is covered with "Bon Ami" (whitewash), used in window cleaning, except the lower foot or two, so that little is visible beyond. There is a long counter up center in front of the shelves with a cash register at the right end. In the right wall a door up R., leading to the rear room of the store. Below this a table with magazines. Stool at L. of counter, another down R.

Displays of fountain pens, ink, pencils, rulers, maps, drawing instruments, etc., on small counter down left below window.

> *Down* R.C. *a trap door and ladder leads to the* *cellar.   The trap is closed.*

AT RISE: COLONEL SMALL, *a gruff old fellow, with metal rimmed glasses, and an iron-bound disposition, is behind the counter up* C., *while the* FRESHMAN *below the counter is fumbling in his pockets for some money.*

SMALL. *(Gruffly)* Well, have you got it?
FRESHMAN. *(Producing half a dollar)*   Yes, here it is. *(Hands it to* SMALL.*)*
SMALL. Thank you. *(Rings up cash register.)*

(MARJORIE BLAKE, *a pretty bob-haired co-ed, enters from street door, speaks cheerily, as* FRESHMAN *turns and meets her.)*

FRESHMAN. Hello, Margie.
MARGIE. Oh, hello, Norrie. (FRESHMAN *exits street door, carrying book.)* Good afternoon, Col. Small.
SMALL. Oh,. what can I do for you?
MARGIE. I'm ready to work this afternoon, if you want me.
SMALL. *(Sharply)* Work? What at? Who sent you? If it's that employment bureau, get out—the last girl couldn't read. Can you read?
MARGIE. Why, yes—I'm a Junior at the University.
SMALL. That don't prove nothin'.
MARGIE. I'm studying to be a librarian. I'm Marjorie Blake, from Professor Griggs' class. I thought he had it all arranged with you for me to work here three afternoons a week.
SMALL. Oh, yes. Professor Griggs, eh? Thought you weren't coming till Monday, but I'm glad you're here. You can start right in. Take off your hat.

(She starts to do so.) Wait a minute—— *(She puts her hat back on.)* This is part of your course, ain't it? Workin' here?

MARGIE. Yes, sir. I get credit for it as practical experience.

SMALL. And you understand I don't pay you for it?

MARGIE. Yes, sir, I understand that.

SMALL. All right. Take it off. *(She does so.)* I need somebody since the Simmins girl *wanted a raise*. Don't say anything to my other clerk, that Miller feller, about working for nothing. *He* might want a raise. He knows a lot about books, but he's a damn fool. Tell him to finish that window. You can put your hat under the counter.

MARGIE. *(Moves behind counter, and puts it away)* Thank you. Now what shall I do?

SMALL. Wait on the customers, when there is any. Prices are marked plain. Can you work the cash register?

MARGIE. Yes, sir.

SMALL. Good. *Don't forget to do it.* In between times, sort them books in that pile there, and put 'em under the right labels. *(Indicates labelled sections in the shelves.)* I'm back in the office mostly. If you want to know anything, ask Miller. He'll be in in a minute. He ain't quite as dumb as he looks. At least I hope not.

MARGIE. Oh, I don't think he's dumb at all.

SMALL. Do you know him?

MARGIE. I met him once, and I thought he was kind of nice. He's a little timid, but then I'm that way myself. Maybe you scare him.

SMALL. Huh! He's scared to start with. *(Moves up to door* R.*)* Of course it's his privilege to look as dumb as he wants to, but he abuses it. *(Exit.)*

(A pile of books, followed by the lower portions of

his body, appear as JOHN MILLER *slowly emerges from the basement through trap door* R.C. *Carefully balancing the huge pile of books, he moves toward the counter, not seeing* MAR-GIE, *as his head is bent over the books. He is twenty-two, lanky, awkward, sensitive face, metal-rimmed glasses and misfit clothes. He is intensely serious and needs a hair cut. His hair has been parted in center, but is very straggly. As the trap door bumps the counter,* MARGIE *starts.*)

MARGIE. Oh! (JOHN *drops the books—they scatter about their feet.*)

JOHN. Oh, I beg your pardon. *(Recognizes* MARGIE.) Oh—have you been waited on?

MARGIE. *(Below* L. *end of counter)* Oh, I'm not a customer. I work here too.

JOHN. Huh?

MARGIE. I'm the new clerk.

JOHN. *(Surprised but resigned)* Oh, then I suppose I'm discharged. Well, it's all right. I expected it. *(Turns to close trap door.)*

MARGIE. Oh, no, you're not. I'm just here part time, and I wouldn't think of taking your place if I could.

JOHN. *(Anxious to reassure her)* Oh, that would be all right. *(Drops the trap door. Begins to pick up books.)* No one would miss me.

MARGIE. I don't believe you remember me. I'm Marjorie Blake, you know.

JOHN. *(Rising quickly, with books in hand)* Oh, yes, I remember you. I just didn't want to presume upon your—well, that you would remember *me*.

MARGIE. Of course I do. *(Begins to pick up books)* It was so nice of you to give me all those specimens that day when our class was out doing

field work. I couldn't tell one weed from another. I'm afraid I'm not much good at botany.

JOHN. *(Shyly)* Oh, yes, you are. You remembered those specimens all right after I showed them to you three or four times. *(Begins to pick up books.)*

MARGIE. What were you doing out there in the country all by yourself?

JOHN. I was looking for a cactus.

MARGIE. A cactus?

JOHN. Yes, it's—it's sandy out there—I often look for them. I found one once.

MARGIE. Well, it was awfully nice of you to help me out.

JOHN. Oh, that's all right. *(Having picked up all but two or three books, he moves over with them to the R. end of counter.)*

MARGIE. *(Timidly trying to keep up the conversation)* I went out there last Sunday to look for —for some specimens. I thought I saw you up on the hill.

JOHN. Yes, I was out there. I thought maybe I'd find you—er—a cactus or something. *(Busies himself with books, embarrassed.)*

MARGIE. I waved to you—didn't you see me?

JOHN. *(Moving center with a smile)* Why, I kind of thought that was you——

MARGIE. But you didn't wave back.

JOHN. Well, I didn't think you *could* be waving to *me*.

MARGIE. Why not?

JOHN. *(Embarrassed)* Oh, nobody ever does— much.

MARGIE. They don't?

JOHN. Oh, I guess I'm not the kind of fellow people wave at.

MARGIE. Well,—I did . . . *(In mutual embarrassment they dive for the one remaining book on*

*the floor, but stop as they almost bump heads. After
a smile of embarrassment they try it again with the
same result. Finally* JOHN *awkwardly kicks the
book a little to the* R., *picks it up, and places it on his
pile at the end of the counter* R. MARGIE *tries to get
the conversation going again as she moves behind* L.
end of counter with books she has picked up) Two
of the other girls who are studying to be librarians
chose the Varsity Store, down at Twelfth Avenue,
but I thought this one would be nicer.

JOHN. *(Looking from his books. Very much
pleased)* You did?

MARGIE. *(Getting very busy with her books)* It's
more convenient—— Col. Small said you ought to
finish cleaning the window.

JOHN. *(With mild indignation)* Why, he just
told me to let them go, and bring up some more
books. I haven't finished yet.

MARGIE. Well, then, tell him so.

JOHN. I'd like to tell him.

MARGIE. Why don't you?

JOHN. *(Convinced of his own abasement)* Aw,
he wouldn't stand for any argument from me.
(Takes several books to table down R. *and arranges
them.)*

MARGIE. I don't like to argue, either—but we
shouldn't let people impose on us.

JOHN. Oh, I don't.

MARGIE. Good.

JOHN. *(Getting brave)* I *tell* him—sometimes—
I will—I'll just show him once, that he can't chase
me around from one thing to another.

(SMALL *enters right, gruffly. Crosses to* R.C., *turns,
sees* MILLER R.)

SMALL. Hey, Miller—I told you to get them
books.

Act I, "The Poor Nut"

JOHN. *(Pointing at them)* I did, Mr. Small.

SMALL. The note books—the leather note books.

JOHN. No, sir, you said to get these language books from the cellar first.

SMALL. *(Furiously) Will you get them note books!*

JOHN. *(As* MARGIE *glances at him. Speaks bravely)* Well, now——

SMALL. *(Savagely)* Well, what?

JOHN. *(Weakening)* Yes, sir. *(Exits* R.*)*

SMALL. *(To* MARGIE, *disgustedly)* He's dumb. *(Exits* R. *importantly)*

*(*MARGIE *sighs and turns to her books at* R. *end of counter as* JULIA WINTERS, *a tall, good-looking, forceful type of girl, about twenty-two, enters,* L. *She is quite well dressed.)*

JULIA. *(Approaching in front of counter)* I beg your pardon—— Why, Margie——

MARGIE. Julia Winters! *(Rushes down center to meet her. They kiss and burst into a cascade of giggles.)* What on earth are you doing in Columbus?

JULIA. We're down with the Wisconsin team for the track meet tomorrow.

MARGIE. Who's we?

JULIA. My room-mate, Angel, and I.

MARGIE. *(As they giggle some more)* Oh, it's so good to see you. You're stouter, aren't you?

JULIA. *(Not so pleased)* Oh, no, I'm thinner.

MARGIE. *(Quickly)* Well, anyhow you look better. *(More giggles, especially from* JULIA.*)* Where are you stopping?

JULIA. At the Sorority House. I've been looking for you all morning. What are you doing here?

MARGIE. *(Sits on counter)* Oh, this is part of my course. Librarian stuff, you know.

JULIA. *(Sits* L. *of* MARGIE*)* Oh, it seems an eternity since we left the old seminary. *(Giggle)* And you would come here to Ohio State.

MARGIE. And you would go to Wisconsin. *(This is a great joke, so they giggle some more.)* Why don't you ever answer my letters?

JULIA. Oh, I've been so busy.

MARGIE. Yes, you popular old thing, getting your picture in all of the papers.

JULIA. Oh, you mean when I was chosen Miss Wisconsin—silly, isn't it?

MARGIE. Yes. (JULIA *looks hurt.)* Oh, no, I think it's great. (JULIA *smiles.)*

JULIA. *(Preening herself)* I didn't want to go into the beauty contest, it seemed so foolish—but they just made me. The papers copied my picture all over the country.

MARGIE. I noticed it said in the paper you were an honor student in psychology, too. That's something new, isn't it? I never knew you to study.

JULIA. *(Enthusiastically)* You don't have to study in psychology. It's fascinating. *(Spies book on counter, picks it up)* Oh, there's the new psycho-analysis. That's a marvelous book, Margie.. It has a wonderful chapter on inferior complex. Have you read it?

MARGIE. No, I've never taken any psychology.

JULIA. Well, you don't know what you're missing. We've got the most wonderful Professor. He just dotes on psycho-analysis. He's a wiz.

MARGIE. Is he good looking?

JULIA. No, but the things he reads in class,—well it isn't like studying at all.

MARGIE. Do you mean—snappy?

JULIA. Snappy? Well—I haven't been able to blush since the first semester,—I'm worn out. *(Giggles. Opens book)* Here's one of the cases we analyzed. This is one of the simplest ones. *(Reads)*

"A woman was unhappily married to a man she had known since childhood. Even worse than this, he had a cork leg. Her most vivid dream was of a small, dark man, walking down stairs, playing a harp, and at the same time selling . . . *watermelons"*—— Well, you know what that means, don't you? *(MARGIE shakes her head. JULIA leans over and whispers in her ear.)*

MARGIE. *(Indignantly)* Why, she ought to be ashamed of herself.

JULIA. You ought to *read*. You'd love Freud. *(Pronounced "Froyd.")* He's so brutal.

MARGIE. Brutal?

JULIA. Brutally frank. He just reduces everything to *Libido*. *(Pronounced "Li-bee-do.")*

MARGIE. What's libido?

JULIA. It's the Life Force—it's what makes you do things.

MARGIE. What sort of things?

JULIA. Oh, you're so naive—you'd better read the book.

MARGIE. *(With a sudden thought)* Say, Julia— how did you know I was here?

JULIA. I didn't. I just came in here to—to look for somebody.

MARGIE. Ah, hah—I heard about you and the captain of the Wisconsin team—*(Giggles)*—what's his name—Hoyt? No wonder you came down to see the meet.

JULIA. Oh, Spike's all right—but I wouldn't want him to find me here. Tell me—is there a fellow working here by the name of Jack Miller?

MARGIE. There's a Miller working here. *(Looks toward door right, doubtfully)* I don't think you would call him Jack. Do you know him?

JULIA. Well,—yes and no. You see we've been corresponding.

MARGIE. Without knowing each other?

JULIA. Uh—huh. *(They just have to giggle over this)* He saw my picture in the paper when I was chosen Miss Wisconsin—you know it was so silly, but the papers copied my picture all over the——

MARGIE. *(Dryly)* Yes, you told me.

JULIA. Oh . . . well, he began to write me the most wonderful letters. He's really a poet—a wonderful poet. He has such a sense of beauty—in one of his letters he called me orchidaceous!

MARGIE. What?

JULIA. Orchidaceous—that means like an orchid.

MARGIE. Well, that sounds like a poet.

JULIA. But Jack isn't a bit like a poet. You know, sort of soft. He couldn't be, being a big fraternity man and a great athlete. *(MARGIE takes another doubtful look toward the door R.)* Let me read you something. *(Takes letter from her handbag, as MARGIE glances at it, she giggles and turns the page)* Here's something I can read. "As I sit here, in my cool study, relaxing after the struggle, tired of the vain cheering of the multitude in the race this afternoon,"—that was the day he won both the sprint and the quarter mile in your All-Ohio meet— *(MARGIE looks puzzled. JULIA continues)* "I wonder if perhaps there may drift before your blue eyes——"

MARGIE. Your eyes are brown.

JULIA. *(Severely)* That's poetic license.

MARGIE. *(Rising from counter)* Oh, that can't be the boy who works here.

JULIA. It must be. There's only this one Miller in the University. I've been dodging Spike all morning, trying to find him.

MARGIE. But you're engaged to Spike Hoyt, aren't you? What would he say?

JULIA. Oh, Spike would throw a fit. *(Giggle)* But it would do him good. He makes me jealous all the time.

(SPIKE HOYT, *an aggressive, athletic youth, enters*
from street door.)

HOYT. Well, Julia, what's the big idea?

JULIA. *(Sweetly)* Oh, hello, Spike. How did
you know I was here?

HOYT. Never mind how I knew you were here.
I asked you what's the big idea?

JULIA. I don't know what you're talking about.
Miss Blake, let me present Mr. Hoyt. (HOYT *moves*
impatiently.) He really isn't always like this, Margie.

MARGIE. How do you do?

HOYT. *(Stiffly)* I'm-very-glad-to-meet-you-I'm-
sure. *(Spoken gruffly and swiftly.)* Julia is supposed to be engaged to me, Miss Blake. You
wouldn't suspect it, though, unless I told you. She
pretended to be all full of anxious to see me in this
track meet, had to follow the team to Columbus.
(Crossing to MARGIE R.C.*)*

JULIA. *(L. of* HOYT*)* Well, if you don't appreciate having me root for you——

HOYT. Oh, yes—you had to come, but not to root
for me—oh, no. It was to run around like a lolly,
asking everybody you see about this Jack Miller.

JULIA. Oh, who told you such a thing?

HOYT. Who didn't tell me? The fellows from
the Psi Sigma House kidded me about your calling
up there.

JULIA. How did they know who called?

HOYT. They said, "Who's speaking?"—and then
like an egg you spoke! . . . And besides that, two
or three *girls* rub it in—you ought to consider *me*.
I used to go to this school and I'm known here.
And then—to make it good, I find you in here looking for him! He works here, doesn't he? *(Turns to*
MARGIE.*)*

MARGIE. There is a Miller here, but it can't be the same one.

HOYT. It better not be. Who is this bird, Julia? It isn't that sap of a John Miller from New Winchester, I hope?

JULIA. He's not a sap—he's a fine boy.

HOYT. Oh, I knew him when he was a Freshman —he's an awful boob. We started in this school together—before I went to Wisconsin. He's still here, eh? He would be, the poor nut.

JULIA. You'll find out if he's a poor nut, when he beats you in the meet tomorrow.

HOYT. I suppose you want me to get beaten.

JULIA. I hope you do.

HOYT. *(Shocked)* What? And you call yourself a Wisconsin girl! Do you want to be a traitor? Wait till I tell them that when we get back!

JULIA. *(Furiously)* Tell them—— You can tell them that I rooted for Ohio State.

HOYT. You wouldn't do *that!*

JULIA. *Yes, I will. I'm going to root for Ohio State.*

HOYT. *(Almost overcome)* I don't care for myself—but—*Wisconsin!* All right—— Go ahead. *(Crosses to door* L.*)* But a fat chance your friend Miller will have to beat me. He isn't even on the team, the poor sap.

JULIA. Don't you dare talk like that. He's a Fraternity Brother of yours. *(She says this with bated breath.)*

HOYT. *(Derisively)* That goof Miller—a Psi Sigma! Listen, woman—at the dinner when I was pledged to Psi Sigma, that oil can spilled noodle soup on himself, and fell in a faint. You can have him! *(Exits furiously, slamming the door.)*

JULIA. Oh, dear—— *(She paces over to the window* L.*, rubs a little spot in the whitewash, and peeps out)* Oh, Margie—those are Angel's feet.

MARGIE. What are?

JULIA. See—outside—— *(She stoops, looks under whitewashed space in window)* "Angel," my room-mate—she's walking away with Spike—— Wouldn't you know it?

MARGIE. Oh, well, let her have him.

JULIA. I will not! We're engaged—and that damn Angel knows it, too. *(She dashes out the door.)*

(JOHN re-enters from R., carrying pile of note books and an apple. He places them in the small bookcase against the wall R.)

MARGIE. *(Who has returned behind counter. Looking at him curiously)* Say, do they ever call you Jack?

JOHN. *(On guard)* What?

MARGIE. I say, do they ever call you Jack?

JOHN. *(Sadly)* No, they never do. . . . .

MARGIE. What do they call you?

JOHN. Well, usually they just point at me. Why?

MARGIE. Oh, I was just puzzled.

(MAGPIE WELCH, the University cheer-leader, a flippant, pleasant little fellow, enters from L. He is followed by "HUB" SMITH, a rather reserved, critical student of the most "standard" type, dressed in the quiet manner. Each carries an armful of books. MAGPIE is dressed in the most extreme collegiate style—flannel shirt, corduroy trousers, etc., a white sailor's hat with names signed all over it.)

HUB. Hello, Margie.

MARGIE. Hello, Hub. Hello, Magpie.

MAGPIE. *(Cheerily)* Hi, Marge—— Hot at the old life-work right off the bat, eh? Imagine taking

a course like that where you have to *work* all the time. I like a course where you can get some sleep.

HUB. Oh, shut, Magpie. Since he's cheerleader, he's got more to say than a radio announcer.

MAGPIE. *(At L. end of counter)* Come on—old Acid Mouth—put your books on the counter and get down to business. *(Drops his own books; HUB likewise.)* The point is: we are badly bent—in need of financial what-nots. Now we have here a splendid collection of books, which we will part with for a mere song!

MARGIE. Where on earth did you get *all those books?*

HUB. *(L. of MAGPIE, innocently)* From the fraternity house—we stole——

MAGPIE. *(Interrupting with a gesture)* They are *our* books. The year's about over and we don't need books any more. These balmy evenings we can't study anyhow. How much will you give us for them?

MARGIE. Well, I can't buy them—maybe Mr. Miller here—— *(JOHN has shrunk back right during this dialogue.)*

MAGPIE. Ah, there, Miller, old kid. Step up and buy.

JOHN. Thank you. I—— Can I look at them first? *(He begins to do so, jotting down prices. Above counter at R. end.)*

MAGPIE. All right, but don't get them dirty. *(Crosses R. JOHN is behind counter, R. of MAR- GIE. HUB in front of counter, L. of MARGIE.)* How come you're not out for track any more, Miller?

JOHN. *(Not looking up)* Oh—I gave it up, after some thought.

HUB. Yes, I noticed you haven't been around for the last week, when I made up the attendance list for Coach. *(JOHN nods diffidently.)*

MARGIE. *(To relieve* JOHN'S *embarrassment)* How do you like being Manager, Hub?

MAGPIE. He's only assistant—don't flatter him.

HUB. *(Airily)* It's all right, but it's a lot of work. What was the matter, Miller? Find you were outclassed?

JOHN. Well, I guess I'd never be much good . . .

MAGPIE. Why, he ran a trial quarter the other day that looked slick. What was the time? *(Turns to* JOHN.*)*

JOHN. Oh, I don't know—when the coach looked at the stop-watch—he gave me a kind of a funny look . . . and so—I just kept on running till I got *home.*

MARGIE. You mustn't be so easily discouraged.

HUB. Why don't you snap out of that attitude, Miller—and do something? Get a hair-cut, for instance?

MAGPIE. *(Putting over one of his best "nifties")* If he got a *hair-cut* he couldn't make Phi Beta Kappa.

HUB. Well, how much for the books?

JOHN. I think we can give you four dollars and fifteen cents for the books.

HUB. *(Forcefully)* I'll sell you the bunch for five dollars—and settle it.

JOHN. All right—— *(Rings up "No Sale" on cash register, stops, looks up suddenly)* No, wait a minute—that's *more!* (HUB *and* MAGPIE *laugh.)* I'm afraid four fifteen is the best—and *that* is speculative, practically.

HUB. *(Stepping up to him)* Now, don't try to take advantage of us.

MAGPIE. *(Stepping up on* R. *side)* Come on, trot out the five.

JOHN. *(Hesitantly)* Well, I guess it's all right. *(Removes five dollar bill from cash register, holds it out)* All right, fellows, thanks.

HUB. *(As both grab for it.* HUB *gets it)* Oh, that's all right. *(Crosses left.)*

JOHN. *(Gathering up the books. To* MARGIE*)* I'll have to file these away on the list in the back office. *(Crosses* R.; *speaks to* MARGIE*)* Will you excuse me?

MAGPIE. *(Emphatically)* With pleasure.

JOHN. Thank you—— *(Sees the point)* Oh— *(Exits* R.*)*

HUB. *(To* MAGPIE*)* So that's the fellow you and Pierce want to take into the fraternity.

MAGPIE. Aw, he means well.

HUB. Blah! *(Changes the subject)* Margie, are you coming up to the house for dinner tonight? You promised, you know.

MARGIE. Well, Julia Winters is in town. She may want me to do something with her.

HUB. Bring her along for Magpie.

MAGPIE. What does she look like? I'm shy of these "blind dates."

MARGIE. Aw, she's a peach, Magpie. You know, she was Miss Wisconsin.

MAGPIE. Oh, well, I wouldn't want to miss Wisconsin. Sure, bring her along.

*(*WALLIE PIERCE, *a good-looking athlete, appears in door, followed by* COACH JACKSON, *a hard-boiled egg of thirty-five or forty.)*

WALLIE. Hello, everybody. *(*MAGPIE *says, "Ah, the Captain of our noble track team!")*

MARGIE. Hello, Wallie.

COACH. *(Ignoring* MAGPIE*)* Thought we saw you come in here, Hub. Get over to the track and make up the list.

HUB. *(Briskly)* Yes, sir.

COACH. And hurry up. Pierce and I have got

troubles of our own today. Come on, Wallie. *(He exits.)*

WALLIE. See you later, Margie. *(Follows.)*

MARGIE. What did Coach mean by "trouble"? Aren't we going to win the meet tomorrow?

HUB. Haven't you heard? Saunders is ineligible.

MARGIE. No! (JOHN *re-enters from* R., *quietly.*)

HUB. Yes! But I told Pierce to try to fix it up with Professor Deming, somehow.

MAGPIE. Aw, shut up. With me leading the cheers, those Badger "bozos" are sunk! *(They exit boisterously. JOHN is behind the counter, R. of MARGIE.)*

MARGIE. They're kind of crazy, aren't they?

JOHN. *(Seriously)* Oh, no, they're *always* like that,—sort of happy and not caring a darn about anything . . . I wish I could be that way.

MARGIE. Oh, Hub's pretty nice, if he is crabby. But you wouldn't want to be like Magpie, would you, honestly?

JOHN. Well, I wouldn't want to wear that kind of a *hat*—but after all they're both Psi Sigmas—and big men in school, almost as big as—as Wallie Pierce.

MARGIE. He was just in here. What's so *wonderful* about Wallie?

JOHN. Why, Pierce is captain of the track team, and Sphinx and Psi Sigma——

MARGIE. Well, *you* are very likely to make *Phi Beta Kappa,* aren't you?

JOHN. Oh, I might, but that isn't like a *social* fraternity, you know.

MARGIE. But it's a great honor to be so good in your school work that you're chosen for it.

JOHN. Oh, sure, but those other fellows don't think so. They just think Phi Beta Kappa men are a lot of long-haired goofs. It's honorary and every-

thing—but not like the honors Wallie Pierce has.

MARGIE. Do you think those things are so important when you get out in life?

JOHN. Well, this is our life now—I'd give anything in the world to be a Psi Sigma—but—I guess I'll wash the window. *(Crosses to door left, picks up a dry cloth from window sill, and begins to rub the Bon Ami from the glass pane in the door.)*

MARGIE. *(Sympathetically)* You don't belong to any fraternity, do you?

JOHN. No, I made up my mind that if I couldn't be a Psi Sigma, I wouldn't be anything. So of course I'm not anything. I guess it's just as well, though. The other fraternities have a hard enough time without me being a burden to them.

MARGIE. *(Sitting on L. end of counter)* I never met anyone like you before.

JOHN. How do you mean?

MARGIE. Oh, you know, so *awfully* modest. Of course, it's a relief after most of these conceited boys—but don't you think you're a little extreme?

JOHN. *(Turning away from his work)* Oh, I'm not modest—I've had some wonderful things happen to me—considering it was *me*. Now just to look at me you wouldn't believe that I have been invited to dinner at the Psi Sigma house, would you?

MARGIE. Oh, I don't know.

JOHN. *(Proudly and tenderly)* Well, I have—twice. Just a couple of weeks ago Wallie Pierce took me up there. He's in the same botany laboratory with me, and he has been very, well—*yes*—you might almost say—friendly.

MARGIE. But you said you were there *twice*.

JOHN. Oh, fortunately, none of them remembered the first time. That was four years ago. There's a new crowd there now. I'd never dare to go if any of the elder fellows were still there. *That* was just

—just terrible! *(Turning to the door, he absent-mindedly draws the Greek letters, "Psi Sigma," in the whitewash with his finger.)*

MARGIE. What was?

JOHN. What happened four years ago. I'd rather not talk about it. *(Overcome by the memory, he turns back to the door, erases the letters "Psi Sigma" and rubs away busily at the glass for a moment. MARGIE turns away, feeling that the subject is closed. After a second JOHN turns toward her again, unable to drop the painful subject)* Oh . . . It was terrible.

MARGIE. *(Sympathetically)* Can't you tell me about it? I'm really interested.

JOHN. Well . . . *(Crosses R. with an apprehensive look toward COLONEL SMALL'S door. Turns back and sits on counter R. of MARGIE.)*

MARGIE. What was so terrible about it?

JOHN. *(Hesitantly)* Well, you see, they had noodle soup.

MARGIE. *(Remembering HOYT's remark)* Noodle soup?

JOHN. Yes, at this dinner at the Psi Sigma House —I was a Freshman, and they were "rushing" me— they really *were*. You see, I had been recommended to them by a friend of my mother's—he didn't know me very well. They were "rushing" another fellow named Hoyt.

MARGIE. Hoyt?

JOHN. Yes. He's at Wisconsin now. Well, we were invited to dinner together. They liked Hoyt, but I was pretty nervous. Well, they had this noodle soup—and they said Grace. We never said Grace at home; my father was a doctor.

MARGIE. *(At a loss to see the connection)* He never said Grace?

JOHN. Well, not after *I* was born. Well, at this

dinner, all of a sudden, I realized that I was eating my soup right in the middle of Grace!

MARGIE. *(Tensely)* Well?

JOHN. *(Proceeding with a morbid fascination)* I went to bow over, and I got my elbow on the edge of my plate, and—immediately I was all covered with noodles! Oh, God, it was awful! *(He almost breaks down at the memory and begins to absently brush himself with the Bon Ami cloth, leaving smudges of white on his clothes, in place of the imaginary noodles.)*

MARGIE. You never got over it, did you? What did you do afterward?

JOHN. Oh, I quit school after a week or so. I couldn't bear it—that soup—and then my father died, too—that was another thing.

MARGIE. But you came back?

JOHN. Oh, yes, after things settled down at home. I worked first for a while, then I heard that Hoyt had gone to Wisconsin, so I came back. . . . I may be able to get both degrees next year.

MARGIE. Your Master's Degree, too? Oh, fine— you could be an instructor then, or something.

JOHN. *(Pleased at this sympathetic attitude)* Yes, I'd like that. You know everybody says teaching doesn't amount to anything, but sometimes I think a fellow might be happier if he just didn't try to amount to anything. You ought to see the paper I'm preparing on the Algae. *(Pronounce "Algy.")*

MARGIE. *(Moving nearer)* The Algae?

JOHN. Yes, and I've got a collection. I'd like to show them to you some . . . some . . . time . . . *(He breaks off, embarrassed; rises)* I'd better clean that window. *(Crosses to door left and resumes cleaning.)*

MARGIE. Oh, wait a minute. I like to talk to you. You're sort of fascinating.

JOHN. *(Looking at her doubtfully)* You don't mean that in earnest?

MARGIE. Yes, I do.

JOHN. *(With an embarrassed grin)* Aw . . . *(Crosses awkwardly and sits on stool L. of counter)* It's easy to talk to you. Most people are so—well, how do you mean, fascinating?

MARGIE. *(Thoughtfully)* Well, you're sort of a dreamer, aren't you? You'd like to be a Psi Sigma, and you went out for the track team—you'd like to be an athlete . . . *(Picks up book on psycho-analysis. Glances at it, then at JOHN thoughtfully)* You know, I was told about a boy once who wanted to do a lot of brave things, and didn't, so he made up stories about himself and pretended that he did them.

JOHN. *(Glancing at her uneasily)* I guess you thought he was kind of a darn fool, didn't you?

MARGIE. *(Smiling reassuringly)* No. I guess he didn't have any friends and he was sort of discouraged, and making up stories was good for him. It made him feel that he was somebody—kept him from going to pieces.

JOHN. *(Sadly)* I know what you mean—— *(Then a little suspiciously)* Of course *I* never did anything like that—*stories*——

MARGIE. Oh, no—but *this* boy used to pretend that he was making love, too. He would write letters and tell all these things he did to an imaginary girl—sort of an ideal.

JOHN. *(Considerably startled by the similarity to his own case)* Well, there wouldn't be any harm in that, would there?

MARGIE. No, not a bit. *(JOHN turns front, reassured.)* Unless it were to a *real* girl. And he made her fall in love with a sort of an ideal of him. *(JOHN seems lost in worried thought.)* You wouldn't want to ruin a girl's life, would you? *(JOHN shakes*

his head absently. MARGIE *slips the question over)*
Do you idealize *her?*

JOHN. *(Absently)* I always imagine she's kind
of delicate—like a flower—you know——

MARGIE. *(Who has connected it all up with*
JULIA's *story)* Orchidaceous!

JOHN. Yes—*how did you know?* (*Rises, startled.*)

MARGIE. Julia Winters was just in here looking
for you!

JOHN. *(Terrified)* What?

MARGIE. She'll be back!

JOHN. Ooo! *(Dashes to trap door, opens it and
begins to descend ladder.)*

(PIERCE *and* PROFESSOR DEMING, *a man about fifty,
enter* L.)

PROFESSOR. Hello, John. (JOHN *stops, halfway
down the ladder.*) How do you do, Miss Blake?

MARGIE. How do you do, Professor Deming?

PIERCE. *(Down* L.*)* Well, John, your Professor
Deming has some good news for you.

PROFESSOR. (L. *of* MARGIE) Yes, John, your
school work has been so fine that, at our Chapter
meeting this afternoon, you were elected to Phi
Beta Kappa.

MARGIE. Oh!

JOHN. *(Still dazed)* What? I was? Well, well.
(Ascends two or three steps.)

MARGIE. Congratulations, Jo—Mr. Miller—— I
don't care what the boys think of Phi Beta Kappa—
I think it's fine.

PIERCE. I just met Mr. Deming, and when he
told me about it I thought we'd just stop in and ask
you to come up to the Psi Sigma House for dinner
tonight.

JOHN. The Psi Sigma House? Well, well, well.
(Comes all the way out of the cellar, delighted.)

PIERCE. Yes, all the fellows will be glad to hear the news. I've got to run over to the track now, but Mr. Deming will go up with you, if you're through here.

MARGIE. Oh, I forgot you're a Psi Sigma, Professor.

PROFESSOR. I try not to forget it. How about it, John?

JOHN. Well, that's wonderful. I'll be glad to come, all right. I'll go ask Col. Small if he wants me to work this evening. *(Starts R.)*

MARGIE. You're not supposed to work in the evenings, are you?

JOHN. No, I'm not supposed to, but I do sometimes. I don't like to argue with him. He's nervous. *(He exits R.)*

MARGIE. *(Looking after JOHN)* Oh, I wish he had some spunk.

PIERCE. That's the trouble; he gets scared. He quit the track squad last week for no reason at all.

PROFESSOR. It's just as well he did. That's not his field, Pierce. He ought to stick to botany; he's brilliant at that—first man to be elected to Phi Beta Kappa this year.

PIERCE. He is, eh? Lord, I used to laugh at Phi Bet when I was a Freshman, but I'd rather have that old scholastic key than all the old college honors put together.

MARGIE. But he wouldn't. He wants to be like you—funny, isn't it? *(PIERCE looks startled at the word "funny.")*

PROFESSOR. *(Crossing down R. to table)* No, it isn't funny, it's rather tragic.

PIERCE. What do you mean, *tragic?*

PROFESSOR. But it's a disease most of us have to go through.

PIERCE. A disease?

PROFESSOR. Yes, the desire for conformity—the

desire to be just like everybody else. It's almost epidemic at present; John has an acute case.

(JOHN *re-enters from* R.)

JOHN. He says I can go most any time now. *(Moves behind cash register, picks up note book.* MARGIE *is behind counter,* L. *of* JOHN, PIERCE *down* L. PROFESSOR *down* R.)

MARGIE. I'm going to dinner at the Psi Sigma house, too.

JOHN. You are?

PIERCE. Yes, and the Wisconsin team got in this morning—their Captain is a Psi Sigma, so I guess he'll be there too—Spike Hoyt.

JOHN. *(Dropping the note book)* Hoyt! *(Turns to* PROFESSOR) Say, I just remembered, I've got a lot of work to do this evening at home.

PROFESSOR. Oh, you can do that afterward.

(JULIA *enters from street door.* JOHN *turns and looks at her, frightened.*)

JULIA. *(Breathlessly)* Oh, Margie——

MARGIE. Oh, did you catch Spike?

JULIA. No, and I can't find Jack, either. *(JOHN slowly bends over until he disappears behind the counter.)* When you get through here, will you help me look for him? It's so strange—I don't know what to think. Oh, are you busy?

MARGIE. *(As she misses* JOHN) This is—Professor Deming, Miss Winters.

PROFESSOR. How do you do?

JULIA. How do you do? *(Turns to* WALLIE PIERCE—*hopefully)* And are *you* Jack Miller? *(PIERCE looks offended.)*

MARGIE. Oh, no, this is Wallie Pierce. Wallie is the Captain of *our* track team.

JULIA. Well, then you can tell me. It's the strangest thing—— (JOHN *crawls out from behind* R. *end of counter, tries to pass the* PROFESSOR, *who does not see him, and blocks his way to the door* R.) I'm looking for one of the men on your team,—Jack Miller.

PIERCE. Miller? Why, he's right here! (JOHN *rises, in panic.*)

JOHN. *No!* (*Tries to get past the* PROFESSOR *unsuccessfully, turns back in desperation.*)

JULIA. (*Looking at* JOHN *aghast*) Are you Jack Miller? (*Unable to speak,* JOHN *makes a sudden dive down the trap door and disappears.*) Is *that* Jack?

MARGIE. That's Jack.

JULIA. Well, the poor nut—he can't get away from me like that. I'm going to tell him a few things. (*She follows him down the ladder, angrily.*)

MARGIE. (*Laughing*) Wait, Julia, I'll go with you. Excuse me. (*She, too, descends the ladder.* PIERCE *and the* PROFESSOR *exchange a look of amazement.*)

PROFESSOR. Well, of all the——

(MAGPIE *and* HUB *rush in from the street door.*)

MAGPIE. Where's Miller?

HUB. Yes, where's Miller?

PIERCE. The girls are chasing him.

HUB. Chasing Miller? What for?

PIERCE. Search me.

MAGPIE. We've just heard he's made Phi Beta Kappa.

PROFESSOR. That's true.

MAGPIE. And the Sig Rhos are looking for him. We need scholarship worse than they do!

PROFESSOR. (*Smiling*) Well, that's one way to get it.

MAGPIE. Our bunch has got to work fast.

PIERCE. Well, how about it, Hub? Everyone has O.K.'d him but you.

HUB. *(L.C.)* Well, we can't let the Sig Rhos get him, but doggone it, I think a fraternity ought to come up to a certain standard, and be a gentleman—

PIERCE. This boy *is* a gentleman.

HUB. *(Feeling that this is the* one *test)* Well, I'd like to get him drunk, and see how he carries his liquor! (MAGPIE *and* PIERCE *nudge him, indicating that the* PROFESSOR *is present.* HUB *looks embarrassed.)*

PIERCE. Well, say something—yes or no?

MAGPIE. Yeah—come on——

HUB. Oh, all right—O.K. But I make one reservation. If we do pledge him, we've got to civilize him. Make him dress and act human, like other people—— *(Adjusts his own necktie, proudly.)*

PROFESSOR. *(R.C.)* But look here. If you boys want to pledge Miller, all right. It will encourage him, and he may be a good influence for you.

HUB *and* MAGPIE. Huh?

PROFESSOR. But try to encourage him to just be himself. Don't force him into the regulation mode. You see he's different from you two boys—he has the old-fashioned idea that college is an educational institution.

HUB. *(Interrupting)* Oh, we know he's a dumb bell—I'll take charge of him.

MAGPIE. Then God help him.

(JULIA *enters from* R., *followed by* MARGIE.)

MARGIE. He got out the back way. (HUB *and* MAGPIE *cough pointedly.)*

PIERCE. Oh, Miss Winters? May I present Mr. Magpie Welch, and Mr. Hub Smith.

JULIA. Oh, how do you do?

HUB *and* MAGPIE. *(Speaking together)* I'm very pleased to meet you, I'm sure. *(They break off and look at each other reproachfully.)*

HUB. *(Stepping forward)* We hear you've been chasing John Miller.

MAGPIE. *(Stepping in ahead of him)* Of course we didn't believe it, but that's the story we heard.

JULIA. *(Playing up to the two new boys)* Huh, I nearly dropped dead when I saw him.

HUB. What did he do?

JULIA. He fell down stairs.

HUB. He would.

PIERCE. You hadn't seen him before?

JULIA. I should say not, and I don't care if I never see him again.

(SMALL pushes JOHN on from R., drowning his protests.)

SMALL. Git in there! What do you mean by picking flowers in the back yard with a store full of customers?

JOHN. *(Who has his hands full of plant specimens, weeds, grasses, flowers and a flat cactus, like a three-branched pancake)* Now listen, please——

SMALL. Git in there! *Wait* on that *lady!* *(Gives* JOHN *a final push, pointing at* JULIA, *and exits* R.)

(JOHN stands confronting JULIA, who is L. of him, PROFESSOR down R., MARGIE at L. end of counter and the three boys down L.)

JULIA. *(With poisonous sweetness)* Were you picking flowers for me, *Jack?*

PIERCE. Oh, you know Miller?

JULIA. Oh, we know each other very well, don't we—*Jack?*

MAGPIE. *Jack?*

JOHN. *(Terribly confused)* Oh, yes, we always call each other Jack—I mean I call her—well—er— you know John is my right name. *(Turns to PROFESSOR helplessly.)*

JULIA. What made you run away?

JOHN. I *knew* you—I mean I didn't recognize you,—er—— *(Turns to PROFESSOR again.)*

PROFESSOR. *(Coming to the rescue)* You mean you hadn't met for some time.

JULIA. No, but we *corresponded*—didn't we, Jack?

JOHN. What? Oh, yes, corresponded. *(Turns to PROFESSOR nervously)* That is, we wrote letters back and forth, occasionally. *(Turns back to JULIA)* Oh, yes, indeed. *(Crosses to PIERCE, desperately)* It's a hot day. *(Wipes brow with plant specimens.)*

PIERCE. *(At L. end of counter)* Seems cool in here—was it hot out in the yard?

JOHN. *(Trying to be nonchalant)* Oh, yes—hot —very hot. *(Attempts to sit on counter. Sits on MARGIE's lap, who is on center of counter. Rises in terrible confusion. Bows to MARGIE.)* I beg your pardon. *(Turns to JULIA, who laughs at him, turns back to MAGPIE and HUB, who are also giving him the laugh. Tries to change the subject)* I thought I could utilize the time to collect a few specimens. *(Indicates flowers, etc., in his hand. The boys snicker and turn away. As JULIA eyes him, he crosses back to PROFESSOR down R., desperately)* Look, Professor. Here's a campanulaceous flower that I've never seen before—and just look at *this*— it's a *cactus!* Yes, sir, a real cactus.

PROFESSOR. *(Not very helpful)* Well, well.

JULIA. *(Moving down L. of JOHN)* Well, what about it?

JOHN. *(Painfully, trying to keep on the subject of cactuses, or anything not personal)* Well, you

know that is not indigenous to this locality, by any means. No, by no means . . .

JULIA. It isn't *what?*

JOHN. What? A cactus. Or certainly of the cactus family. *(Pricks finger)* It is prickly.

MAGPIE. (L. *of* PIERCE) You said it was hot out there. Maybe it has prickly heat.

JOHN. *(Unable to cope with levity)* Well . . . no——

JULIA. When do you athletes get time to study up all these words, John?

MAGPIE *and* HUP. Athletes?

JOHN. Words? Oh, perhaps I was a rifle pedantic—but I always thought I had a very poor vocabulary—except . . . *(Drops all his specimens except cactus on bookcase—or table down* R.*)*

PROFESSOR. *(Rising)* Don't let them worry you, John. It wouldn't harm any of you boys to enlarge your vocabularies a little. Now I'm going to walk on up to the house, if you'll excuse me. (PROFESSOR *crosses toward door* L. JOHN *follows, hanging on his arm.)*

PIERCE. Certainly. See you at dinner, Professor.

JOHN. But, Professor, about this cactus.

PROFESSOR. We'll look into that cactus later, John. *(Turns to* MAGPIE *and* HUB *down* L.*)* You know, boys, if you have the right viewpoint, the cactus can be just as thrilling as a football game. (PROFESSOR *exits up* L.*)*

JOHN. *(Starts to exit door* L.*)* Say, I think I'll just go along with him. I need to get cleaned up a little.

JULIA. *(Going right after him)* No, Jack—you aren't afraid to stay and tell *me* about your specimens, are you?

JOHN. Oh, no—only I didn't think you would be interested.

JULIA. Well, I am. *(She sits decidedly; rises with a howl)* Ouch, I sat on it!

MARGIE. On what?

JULIA. On his damn cactus! *(Pulls it off her dress; throws it on floor. ALL laugh.)*

JOHN. *(Picks it up; examines it)* It's all right—you didn't hurt it.

JULIA. I don't care if I killed it—look what it's done to me! *(She moves down L., pulling her skirt around.)*

JOHN. No! *(Crosses R. behind counter—dropping cactus near cash register.)*

MARGIE. You aren't bleeding or anything.

JULIA. No, but I'm stabbed. My dress is all full of little stickers, too.

MARGIE. *(Moving L.)* I'll help you pick them out. *(JOHN tries to sneak out R.)*

HUB. *(Turning JULIA around so he can get a better look)* Here—the light's better there.

JULIA. Jack's the one that did it—let him pick them out. *(JOHN straightens up, horrified at the idea.)*

JOHN. Ohh!

MAGPIE. Sure, he can do it right.

HUB. *(Crossing to JOHN; pushes him L.)* Sure, step up, John, and help the lady.

JOHN. *(Piteously)* It isn't really my cactus—I just found it.

JULIA. Well, come here and take it back—I've still got half of it in my skirt.

(HUB *pushes* JOHN *down beside* JULIA. MARGIE *is on her* L., *as is* MAGPIE. HUB R. *of* JOHN. JOHN *timidly attempts to pick out one or two cactus spines.)*

JULIA. Don't push—pull! *(PIERCE crosses R. behind counter, grinning.)*

Act I, "The Poor Nut"

JOHN. *(Turning to* HUB*)* Oh, listen. I'm no good at a thing like this.

HUB. Well, what do you think we are—professionals?

MAGPIE. I'll bet he's done this before and won't admit it.

HUB. Sure—I saw him yesterday noon chasing a couple of girls with a cactus in each hand.

JOHN. *(Desperately)* No—those were overshoes! *(The boys shout with laughter.)*

MARGIE. I think we've got them all out now. *(*JOHN *immediately jumps up and backs away.)*

MAGPIE. That's great, John. *(He and* HUB *applaud.)*

JULIA. I don't think it's so funny. I should think you boys would be ashamed to have a cactus hound as a member of your fraternity.

HUB. *(Suspiciously)* What do you mean—a member of our fraternity? He doesn't belong to it yet.

JOHN. *(Desperately)* No, of course not. That was just one of her little jokes. *(Tries to smile at* HUB, *then at* PIERCE. *Crosses* R., *hopelessly, feeling that the worst has come.)*

JULIA. Oh, no, I'm not joking. I was under the impression that you were a member.

PIERCE. *(Sensing that rescue is needed)* We were just going to talk to John about that.

JULIA. What do you mean?

PIERCE. I mean I was just going to ask John something. *(Turns to* JOHN*)* It's about the fraternity. *(*MAGPIE *moves in* L. *of* PIERCE.*)* Of course, you know, we don't usually do any "rushing" at this time of year, but well, the boys all like you very much, Miller, and we want you to be one of us.

JOHN. What?

PIERCE. Now, here's a pledge pin I'd like to put

on you, if you feel that you want to say yes. *(Takes pledge button from pocket.)*

MARGIE. *(Softly to* JULIA*)* Oh, isn't that wonderful! *(*JULIA *looks stunned.)*

JOHN. *(Pathetically)* Say, Pierce, don't kid me like this. I might believe it or something.

PIERCE. I'm not kidding. Shall I put it on, or do you want to think it over for a while? *(Begins to fasten button in* JOHN'S *lapel, without waiting.)*

JOHN. Oh, no, but I think you fellows ought to think it over.

PIERCE. Oh, rot—we're satisfied—if you are. Here—— *(Shaking hands with* JOHN*)* Congratulations, John—we're mighty glad to have you.

MARGIE. I'm so glad.

MAGPIE. *(Rushing down)* Congratulations, John. *(He shakes hands with* JOHN *and slaps him on back.)*

HUB. *(Shaking hands)* Can't you smile a little?

JOHN. *(Looks at pin proudly; smiles happily; sobers as he looks up)* I'm afraid you fellows are making a terrible mistake!

JULIA. I quite agree. They are! *(Starts to sit on stool* L.E.; *looks hastily to see if cactus is there.)*

PIERCE. We don't think so.

HUB. *(Crossing* R. *to* JOHN, *leans against bookcase—down* R.*)* Well, it's too late to worry about that now. We've got to get you fixed up. You can't go to dinner looking like that. *(Eyes* JOHN'S *appearance disapprovingly.)*

MARGIE. *(Up* L.*)* Oh, don't be so funny, Hub—that's mean.

HUB. *(Grinning at* MARGIE*)* Why not? He's a freshman. *(Turns to* JOHN *sternly)* You understand that, don't you, Miller? Even though you're a junior in school, you're a freshman in the fraternity and from now on you're going to be treated like one. Understand?

JOHN. Oh, I don't mind that.

HUB. All right. Then I'll take you in hand. Now in the first place, you've got to begin to look human.

JOHN. Right away? I've always looked like this.

MAGPIE. (L. of HUB) Oh, he doesn't mean completely human—just like him. Order your suits from Tripler's.

JULIA. He'll have to do more than that to make him look human.

HUB. (Considering) Well, he could smoke a pipe—it might offset the goggles.

JOHN. Mr. Small has one here somewhere. (Hurries to cash register, rings "No Sale" and removes an old pipe from the cash register. The boys laugh.)

HUB. Never mind. We'll begin on your hair and your necktie tonight.

JOHN. (Feeling for it) I have a necktie on.

MAGPIE. Oh, is that what that is? (Tie should be an old black bow tied as a four-in-hand.)

HUB. And your hair—don't you ever comb it?

JOHN. (Proudly) Oh, yes, every morning.

JULIA. That's the way it looks.

HUB. Now you get busy and comb it. Part it on the side the way I do.

JOHN. All right, sir. (Rings up ten cents on the cash register and removes small mirror and comb. Begins to comb his hair. The boys exchange a look of amusement.) Oh, look, now I rang up ten cents!

MARGIE. (To HUB) Well, if you don't like his necktie, can't you lend him another one?

HUB. (Hesitantly) Sure, I'll be glad to. (Crosses to PIERCE—L.C.) Pierce, you just bought a lot of neckties. Can't you lend him one?

PIERCE. Certainly. I'll give him one,—of yours. (Crosses to door L.) I've got to get over to the track.

MARGIE. (Who has been down L.) I'll go with

you and bring the tie back. (PIERCE *and* MARGIE *exit.*)

MAGPIE. (R. *of* JOHN) Hurry up with your hair, Miller.

JOHN. It won't part right. I have a cow lick.

JULIA. You *would* have. (JULIA *sitting on stool down* L.C.)

HUB. (*Slapping counter*) Look here, Miller. Don't argue!

MAGPIE. No!

HUB. (*Crossing to* MAGPIE—*turns back to* JOHN) We've got a lot of work to do on you to try to make you look like a Psi Sigma.

JOHN. I *know* it—— Oh, I get so nervous every time I look in the mirror—— (*Dropping comb nervously*) I'm afraid it's no use, fellows—you'd better take this pin back. I'll never amount to anything.

JULIA. (*Suddenly*) Ah!

MAGPIE. What's the matter? What is it?

JULIA. (*Rising*) I know what's the matter with him, and I can cure him. It isn't his hair or his necktie or his collar—it's nothing external—it's internal, and I can cure him. Come here, Jack!

JOHN. (*Moving slowly* L. *Hypnotized*) I feel all right.

JULIA. Sit down! (*Pushes him on the stool,* L. *of counter*) Oh, I'm so glad I've discovered it. This boy has an inferiority complex.

JOHN. What?

JULIA. The trouble with you is—you have an inferiority complex.

JOHN. I have? That's a bad thing, isn't it?

JULIA. (*Assuming a professional manner*) Terrible, it's the *worst* mental condition *possible*.

JOHN. That sounds as if I would have it, all right.

HUB. How do you know all this, Miss Winters?

JULIA. I've specialized in psychology. *(Steps back and surveys* JOHN *critically)* Something has *impeded the natural functioning of your ego.*

JOHN. *(Swallowing)* What?

JULIA. You are oppressed by a sense of inferiority—helplessness, *futility—aren't you?* I've studied all about you. To begin with, you are an *emotional introvert.*

MAGPIE. And that's only the *beginning.*

JULIA. That is the psycho-analytical name for his psychic type. It is the type which produces most of the extreme neurotic and hysterical cases.

JOHN. *(Running his finger around his collar)* You know this wouldn't make me so nervous if I just had my collar on. *(Turns up coat collar.)*

JULIA. That can wait, but the emotional introvert class also includes many great geniuses.

JOHN. Isn't there some other class I could belong to?

JULIA. Yes, but you *don't.* I can prove it. Take, for example, those *letters.*

JOHN. *(In agony)* Oh, I was afraid you were going to bring that up——

MAGPIE. *(Eagerly curious)* What letters?

JULIA. Never mind, that's between Jack and me. But those letters show what you want to be, and what you can be if you get rid of this complex. Those letters were an attempt to rise above your inferiority, but that is not the right way. The right way is to *remove* your *real inferiority.*

JOHN. *(Gloomily)* You mean shoot myself?

JULIA. Oh, no! *(The boys laugh.)* By conquering your weaknesses and gaining strength, I will help you. I will become your *analyst.*

HUB. *(Seriously interested)* What?

JULIA. I mean his psycho-analyst. *(Crosses to counter)* Where's that book? *(Picks up psychology*

book) Now you boys wait outside. I've got to ask John some very *personal questions.*

JOHN. Oh, no—let them stay!

HUB. *(Crossing L.)* Yes, let us stay.

MAGPIE. *(Crossing L.)* Aw, we don't want to go *now.*

JULIA. *(Pushing them)* No, the relation between a subject and his analyst is very confidential. Now get out. *(Pushing HUB out.)*

MAGPIE. *(At door)* It doesn't sound decent to me. Listen, Julia. Don't tell him there isn't any Santa Claus. *(He exits.)*

(JULIA *crosses to* JOHN, *who has backed over to stool in front of bookcase down* R. *She takes the other stool and sits* L. *of him.)*

JULIA. *(Eagerly enthused)* Oh, Jack, I've always wanted to analyze somebody, and now I've got you. Spike won't let me—he resists me, but I know you *yield* to me.

JOHN. How do you mean—yield?

JULIA. It is a relation in which you must confide in me all your secrets, and that should be easy because you've already idealized me in your mind and in your *letters,* haven't you, Jack?

JOHN. *(Hesitantly)* Oh, yes.

JULIA. *(Deliberately)* Well, first you must tell me all your *sexual problems.*

JOHN. *(Rising, startled)* What?

JULIA. *(With dignity)* Why, Jack, you're a scientific student. You aren't *afraid* to use the word *sex,* are you?

JOHN. No, not in the class-room—but privately it sounds so kind of . . . public. *(Sits again slowly.)*

JULIA You must tell me all your thoughts. Your *libido* must be turned *outward.*

JOHN. Outward?

JULIA. I'm sorry, but it's necessary. *(Then very significantly)* Tell me, Jack, do you *dream* much?

JOHN. *(Nervous)* You mean—when I'm *asleep?*

JULIA. Of course! Now you must tell me *every single dream you've ever had.*

JOHN. *(Rising in indignation)* I beg your pardon!

JULIA. Ah, I thought so! You *must* tell me. It's the only way to delve into your unconscious.

JOHN. My what? *(Buttons his coat nervously.)*

JULIA. Your unconscious mind. The place where you bury all your *evil thoughts* and *hidden longings.*

JOHN. How do you know I *have* any?

JULIA. I can see that there is some dream which *pursues* you. *(JOHN winces.)* *Clings* to you, *frightens you.* *(JOHN shudders. She speaks quickly now as in a "third degree")* What is it?

JOHN. *(Dropping on the stool)* I don't like to talk about it.

JULIA. Come now, *tell Julia*—what is it?

JOHN. Well,——

JULIA. Well?

JOHN. It's *noodle soup.*

JULIA. *(Starts back)* What?

JOHN. *(Aghast)* *Noodle* soup.

JULIA. Noodle soup?

JOHN. Does that mean something bad?

JULIA. Bad? Oh, my God, it's terrible! *(As JULIA backs away, MARGIE enters from up L. hurriedly with tie and collar.)*

MARGIE. Wallie sent you this tie.

JULIA. *(Impatiently)* Oh, Margie, I told those boys to let us alone.

MARGIE. Well, they thought he'd need this, and I thought you'd like this flexible collar.

JOHN. *(Crossing to MARGIE, thankfully, takes collar and tie and starts R. hurriedly)* Oh, thank you—I'll be right out.

JULIA. That's a bow tie—can you tie a bow?

JOHN. Well, not very well. (JULIA *starts toward him.*) Oh, yes, I can. (*Starts* R.)

JULIA. Wait, I'll tie it for you. I knew you were the type who couldn't tie a bow tie. (*As she begins to tie,* SPIKE HOYT *enters from door up* L.)

SPIKE HOYT. (*Sarcastically*) Oh, Julia. (*All three turn.* JOHN *looks scared.*) If you're not too busy there with your *friend*— (JOHN *edges away.*) —I'd like to speak to you a minute.

JULIA. Why, certainly, Spike. Come in.

HOYT. Out here! (*Beckons her toward door* L.)

(JOHN *tries to keep his back turned to* HOYT *and busily buttons the collar on, being plainly nervous in* HOYT'S *presence.*)

JULIA. Oh, all right. Well, what's wrong with *you?* (*Exits with* SPIKE HOYT *up* L.)

MARGIE. (*Turning back to* JOHN) I'll tie it for you. (*Begins to do so.*)

JOHN. (*Looking over her shoulder toward door* L.) He looks bigger than he used to.

MARGIE. It's the underneath and that's shorter, but only an inch or so. (*Looking after* JULIA) She's a peach, isn't she?

JOHN. (*Removes newspaper clipping from pocket. Looking at picture thoughtfully*) Yes, she certainly is!

MARGIE. What's that?

JOHN. Her picture—Miss Wisconsin.

MARGIE. Where did you get it?

JOHN. Out of the newspaper—I bought eleven of them—they wear out so fast! She *is* beautiful. (*Looks at picture.*)

MARGIE. She has such pretty eyes.

JOHN. Yes, blue.

MARGIE. No, they're brown.

JOHN. Oh, well . . . I always *imagined* they were *blue*.

MARGIE. Oh, no—they're a beautiful dark brown—haven't you *noticed* them?

JOHN. Well . . . yes . . .

MARGIE. I wish I had eyes like hers. *My* eyes are *blue*.

JOHN. *(Surprised)* They are? *(Looks at her thoughtfully)* Yes, sir, they are blue, aren't they? Sort of a soft . . . blue. Well—what do you know about that?

MARGIE. I think Julia's awfully interested in you.

JOHN. *(Worried)* She's going to turn my libido outward.

MARGIE. *(Puzzled)* What for?

JOHN. *(Innocently troubled)* Just so she can look at it, I guess.

MARGIE. No, it isn't just that—she likes you.

JOHN. Oh—how could a girl who is beautiful and popular and everything ever like *me?*

MARGIE. Why couldn't she? *(He looks doubtful.)* How would you feel if it you found out she does care for you—better than Spike Hoyt, or anyone?

JOHN. *(Looks at picture)* Oh, Lord, I couldn't bear it!

MARGIE. What!

JOHN. *(Sincerely)* I mean it would be too wonderful! Oh, Lord, I would just feel—— *(Sighs in imagined ecstacy)* You know I'm not always quiet—like you have seen me. Sometimes when something nice happens I get all . . . joyful . . . you know . . . sort of ecstatic!

MARGIE. You mean—if she kissed you, for instance?

JOHN. Oh, such a thing couldn't happen—unless she just meant to renounce everything.

MARGIE. How do you mean?

JOHN. Oh . . . a kiss always seemed just the same to me as getting married.

MARGIE. Why, haven't you *ever* been *kissed?*

JOHN. (*Evading that embarrassing point*) Well . . . *I've* always been more interested in *botany* . . .

(JULIA *enters, followed by* HOYT *angrily.* HUB *and* MAGPIE *follow* HOYT, *grinning.*)

HOYT. Well, Julia, are you coming with me, or aren't you?

JULIA. I'm going to the Psi Sigma house with Jack, as I told you.

HOYT. With Jack! (*Crosses to* JOHN R., *threateningly*) Well, Miller, I never expected to meet you in the Psi Sigma house again.

JOHN. (*With a weak smile*) Oh, hello, Hoyt.

JULIA. Have you been there together before?

HOYT. Oh, yes, indeed. Miller used to be more bashful in those days. He wasn't such a lady's man. (JOHN *is unable to answer.*)

MARGIE. Oh, John wasn't a member of the *fraternity, then.*

HOYT. A member of *what* fraternity?

MAGPIE. Why, we just pledged him. Note the button.

HOYT. (*Looking at* JOHN, *as* JOHN *fingers lapel proudly*) No. Well, he must have changed since I knew him.

JULIA. Oh, well, when you knew him, he wasn't such a great athlete.

JOHN. What? (JULIA *gives him the high sign over* HOYT's *shoulder.*)

JULIA. I've just been telling Spike what a wonderful athlete you are *now*, Jack.

JOHN. Oh, yes . . . I suppose I have changed. (*As* HOYT *looks at him, he puts his foot carelessly*

on the top of the stool, missing it the first time, but making finally what he considers a dandy gesture.)

JULIA. I attribute it to the influence of athletics.

HOYT. *(Interested)* So you really go out for athletics, eh?

MARGIE. Oh, yes, football season is no more than over until he's into basketball——

HOYT. *(Turning to* JOHN, *respectfully)* You play football *and* basketball?

JOHN. Oh, yes. *(Taking pipe from his pocket, he sticks it in his mouth with nervous jauntiness.)*

HOYT. Well, well, well. Julia had an idea you were on the track squad too, Miller. Think you'll get in any of the events tomorrow?

JOHN. *(Lighting pipe, and puffing rapidly)* Oh, three or four. Can't get out of it.

HOYT. Three or four—and you're smoking? Don't you train?

JOHN. Oh, this is just a *pipe. (Coughs—choking on the smoke, but furtively.)*

MAGPIE. *(Enjoying* HOYT'S *astonishment)* You oughtn't to go in too many races, John—you might get tired.

MARGIE. *(Prompting him)* Why, he *won* four or five races in the All-Ohio—didn't you, John?

JOHN. *(Wiping his lips with kerchief)* Oh, that was nothing—I would have won the half mile, too—only a fellow got in front of me—and I didn't want to spike him.

HOYT. *(Impressed)* Is that so!

MARGIE. How do they come to call you "Spike," Mr. Hoyt? (JOHN *feels a little sick, so he bites the apple.)*

HOYT. Oh, that's unfair to me, Miss Blake—they hung that name on me because I spiked a couple of men last year—but it wasn't my fault—they cut in front of me, just as you said, Miller. But you were

a sap to pull up—I wouldn't let anybody butt in front of me—if I had to cut him to pieces!

JOHN. *(Trembling inwardly)* You wouldn't, eh?

HOYT. No! They're supposed to be a full stride ahead before they cut in. But nobody ever *gets* a full stride ahead of *me!*

JOHN. Do you hold them?

HOYT. No—I *out-run* them! And when these fellows tried to cut in and box *me*—I just spiked them, and jumped over them—and I was well within my rights.

(JOHN *is beside bookcase down* R. HOYT L. *of him,* MARGIE, JULIA, HUB *and* MAGPIE *grouped in front of counter up* L.C., *so that neither* HOYT *nor* JOHN *see* COACH JACKSON *and* PIERCE *enter at this point from door up* L. *As they join the group,* MAGPIE *nudges them, and signals silence. They quietly draw back and listen.)*

JOHN. *(Swallowing)* You just . . . spiked them . . . and jumped over them, heh? (HOYT *nods vigorously.)* Both at once?

HOYT. No, in two different races.

MARGIE. Oh, John spiked two of them in the *same* race.

MAGPIE. Sure, one with each foot.

HOYT. What? *(Turns back to* JOHN *suspiciously)* Say, listen.

JOHN. *(Nervously)* One of them fell down, and I stepped on him—and kicked the other one. When I get in a race, I just feel that nothing can stop me. *(The* COACH *leans forward.)*

HOYT. *(Wisely)* Well, then why didn't you win that half mile when the fellow got in front of you?

JOHN. He *fell* in front of me—and I didn't want to step on his head. (HOYT *nods agreement with*

this humanity.) I was afraid I'd get my spikes
stuck.

HOYT. Say, are you trying to kid me?

JULIA. Why, no, Mr. Hoyt. Don't you think
any other boy can spike people beside you?

HOYT. I didn't speak to you, Miss Winters.

MAGPIE. There's a loving engaged couple for
you.

HOYT. (*Furiously*) Engaged? Where do you
get that stuff! That's *all off,* isn't it, Julia?

JULIA. (*Rising to the situation*) Well, I should
say so—that's *ancient history.* Isn't it, Jack?

JOHN. Huh? . . .

HOYT. (*Stepping closer to* JOHN) Oh—so it's
Jack, is it? Well, I've got a few words to say to
you, Jack——

COACH. (*Stepping forward between the two*)
Just a minute there, boys—— I'm glad to hear that
you're so determined about winning all your races,
Miller.

JOHN. (*Looking at him, turns pale. After a
pause he says*) Oh . . . hello . . . Coach. When
did you come in? (*Drops on table down* R.)

COACH. (*Sternly*) How does it come you haven't
been out on the track for practice this week, Miller?

JOHN. Why, I didn't think I needed it.

HOYT. (*Furiously*) What? Say, listen——
(*Starts toward* JOHN. COACH *stops him.* JOHN
grabs stool and points the legs toward HOYT *defen-
sively.*)

COACH. Keep still. Don't get this fellow mad.

JOHN. What? Oh, no, don't get me mad. (*Drops
stool; puts pipe in mouth.*)

COACH. (*Turning to* JOHN) Now, here, just because you run all those races and spiked all those
men is no sign that you can quit training. We have

a meet tomorrow. Put down that pipe! (JOHN *hastily does so.*)

HOYT. (*Grabbing the* COACH's *hand*) Say, Coach, I'm Hoyt—Captain of Wisconsin, and I want to know if this bird is kidding me. He told me he was going to run in six races tomorrow.

COACH. (*Enjoying his bombshell*) He's going to run, all right—and he's going to run against *you!*

JOHN. Yes—— (*Then realizing what* COACH *said*) What?

COACH. I say you're going to run against him in the quarter mile and the relay. I guess two quarters will be enough for you, won't it, John?

JOHN. Well, I—— (COACH *glares.*) Yes, I guess so. (*Drops on stool; munches apple desperately.*)

HOYT. I'll say two races will be enough for you, Miller, if you're going to run against me. And remember what I said about *cutting in.* I wasn't kidding!

(*WARN Curtain.*)

PIERCE. (*Takes* HOYT *by the arm; leads him up to door*) It's dinner time. Come on, Hoyt. Bring the girls, fellows.

HOYT. I'm telling you straight, Pierce, if that fellow gets in my way—I'll murder him! (PIERCE *and* HOYT *exit up* L.)

JOHN. (*Rising nervously*) You were just joking, weren't you, Coach?

COACH. No, I wasn't. Saunders is ineligible, and Jenkins pulled a tendon today.

JOHN. But I won't be any use to you. You'd be much better off without anybody. I'll just be trampled all over the track.

COACH. I'm the one to decide that. Why, you ran a trial four-forty in fifty-three the other day, and then you quit practice!

JOHN. *Fifty-three!* Well, I won't be able to run

it that fast *tomorrow*—I feel kind of *sick*. *(Nervously bites the apple.)*

COACH. Put that apple down! Runners don't eat between meals.

JOHN. Excuse me. I just wanted to get the bad taste of that pipe out of my mouth. *(Tries to hand the apple to* COACH.*)*

COACH. *(Pushing it away)* I don't want the damn thing. *(*JOHN *turns away, standing in front of stool down* R.*)* Just go in tomorrow the way you told Hoyt. Just feel that nothing can stop you! *(He slaps* JOHN *a terrific jolt on the back.* JOHN *drops on stool.* COACH *crosses up* L.*)* So long, fellows.

HUB *and* MAGPIE. *(Speaking together)* So long, Coach. *(*COACH *exits.)*

MAGPIE. Come on, John. We'll tell the bunch all about it. You're the hot stuff tonight—we're proud of you. *(*MAGPIE *exits.)*

HUB. *(At the door)* Yes, and you know who got you into this crowd, don't you? *(Pats himself on the chest and exits.)*

MARGIE. *(At the door)* Hurry, John, they're waiting for us. *(Follows* HUB.*)*

JULIA. *(Who has waited* C.—*speaks tensely)* Jack—did you hear what Spike said?

JOHN. *(Moving toward her)* He said he's going to murder me.

JULIA. I mean to me—about our engagement. You've got to get even with Spike Hoyt for me—for us both! Don't you see—it's all coming through —all that you wrote about yourself in your letters. You are a Psi Sigma now, and a track man. Jack, I'm going to give you something to fight for. I'm going to promise you something. I've been engaged to Spike Hoyt, but if you beat him in the race tomorrow, I'll be engaged to *you*—— *(*JOHN *looks startled.)* Kiss me, Jack.

JOHN. *(Pulling away as* JULIA *grabs his arm)*
Oh, wait, now—you ought to have time to think!

(MARGIE re-enters up L. in time to see this embrace.)

MARGIE.   Coming?—Oh, excuse me.   *(Turns
slightly down L.)*
JULIA. *(Still holding* JACK*)* It's all right, dear.
Tell her, Jack.
JOHN. *(Confused and unhappy)* Yes, it's per-
fectly proper, I guess. We're engaged—practically.
MARGIE. *(Showing her disappointment—but ris-
ing to the situation)* Oh, that's wonderful, isn't it?
JULIA.   Uh-huh.
JOHN. *(Painfully)* Yes. I'm so *happy*——
*(*JULIA *kisses* JOHN *emphatically. He tries to smile,
then bites the apple, and munching it, keeps on trying
to smile as the curtain falls.)*

CURTAIN

(Act plays fifty-three minutes. Do not cut, as other
two acts are short.)

ACT II

SCENE I: *The Trainer's tent. Athletic Field. A shallow tent, with flaps for entrance left. A rubbing table center, R. of it a smaller table with bottles of liniment and a couple of camp stools. Blankets, sweaters and towels scattered about.*

NOTE: *This tent can be hauled up into the flies for an almost instantaneous change to Scene II, using same groundcloth as "the track."*

AT RISE: *We hear crowd in cellar singing as follows:*

Song, "On, Wisconsin." Time, "March On, Wisconsin." Sung by the crowd in cellar under stage. The beginning of the song is cue for rise of curtain.

Doc fills in with business of "rubbing" all through song.

"On, Wisconsin, on, Wisconsin, fight on for your fame,
Run the ball around Ohio, glorify our name.
On, Wisconsin, on, Wisconsin, fight on for your name,
Fight, fellows, fight! fight!! fight!!! and win this game.
Yea——! Yea——!! *Wis-con-sin!!!*

ANNOUNCER. *(Offstage L.)* Result of the pole vault. Pole vault: First, Mitchell of Wisconsin.
CROWD. *(In cellar)* Yea!
ANNOUNCER. Second: Thomas of Wisconsin.

55

CROWD. Yea!

ANNOUNCER. Third: Virgus of Ohio State. Height, eleven feet seven inches.

CROWD. Hurray!

("Doc" SPURNEY, *a gruff, sunburned Irishman, is rubbing one of the Ohio State runners, who lies on the rubbing-table, center, with some liniment. Two or three athletes standing around. This announcement follows immediately on finish of song, "Wisconsin."*)

(*There is the sound of a megaphone off at a distance, announcing the result of the pole vault. The voice is muffled. It is followed by a few weak cheers for Wisconsin. "Doc" cocks one ear trying to make out the announcement, but continues kneading the boy's legs. The boy half rises to listen.*)

DOC. (*Slaps him*) Lay down, there!

PIERCE. (*Entering from R. through tent flap*) Hello, Doc. Can I get a rub? (PIERCE *is in track suit with Ohio on shirt and number ten on his back.*)

DOC. Sure, Wallie. What was that last?

PIERCE. Wisconsin got first and second in the pole vault.

DOC. The Hell they did! (*Slaps his man, and pushes him off table.*)

(*The* MAN *drops back with the others.* PIERCE *slides on the table.* MEN *exit L. with ad lib. talk.*)

PIERCE. Yep. We're still five points ahead, though—and there's the high jump and the relay left.

DOC. When I was out there just now Wisconsin

was winning all three places in the high jump. Our
fellows were jumping like they had on lead pants.
What is it, your legs?

PIERCE. Yes. . . . They'll be calling the relay
pretty soon.

DOC. *(Beginning to rub his legs)* You're trying
to do too much, Wallie. Those hurdles are hard
races. . . . Coach shouldn't have put you in the
hundred, too. I can't keep you men in shape if he's
going to work you to death. *(Slaps* WALLIE'S *leg
impatiently.* PIERCE *winces.)*

PIERCE. We needed the points, Doc.

DOC. Well, you've got your share—thirteen points
—and now you're goin' in the relay! *(Another
slap.)*

PIERCE. We've just got to win the relay! If
Wisconsin cops everything in the high jump we'll be
four points behind.

DOC. Yep—it all depends on the relay now—and
I don't like it with that Miller in there to gum things
up! *(Another slap.)*

PIERCE. Well, don't take it out on *me!* Oh,
Miller can run, Doc—he did pretty well to get second against Hoyt in the four hundred and forty.

DOC. *(Rubbing away)* He can run, but he's got
no guts! *(Attempts another slap at* PIERCE'S *knee,
but* PIERCE *drops and he misses.)* Second, is it?
He could have had first if he hadn't let Hoyt scare
him.

PIERCE. Oh, now, Doc—you know we didn't
really expect him to score anything!

DOC. I know it. And I don't expect it now.
There's no second place in the *relay*—it's first or
nothing! *(Band record on phonograph off stage* L.,
"Ohio and across the field.") You will run No. 4,
won't you?

PIERCE. No. Coach wants me to run first, and
Miller last.

Doc. What for?

Pierce. He figures John lost his nerve when Hoyt came alongside him in the four hundred and forty, and he thinks he'll run better if we give him a lead and get him out in front.

Doc. Well, maybe he will—if he don't see his shadow!

(Magpie, *with megaphone, etc., and* Coach *enter with* John. *One has each arm. He looks dejected. Wears track suit with old "sweat shirt" over it, and glasses.)*

Coach. *(Pushing* John *center)* Come in here and get a rub. They'll be calling the relay soon.

John. Haven't you got someone else you could put in that relay?

Coach. For the last time—*no we have not*—and you'll be all right if you just *run*—and don't let me catch you looking around, the way you did in the four hundred and forty!

John. I didn't look around—Hoyt came up beside me.

Coach. And you politely let him pass you! You weren't all in—I know damn well you weren't!

Magpie. *(*l. *of* Coach) You ran better than anybody thought you could, at that, John.

Coach. That's no excuse for quitting! When a man gets in a race we expect him to run better than we expect him to!

Pierce. *(Rising from table)* What was the matter, John? When he pulled up to you, you didn't seem to try—you just dropped back.

John. Why . . . I thought he was going to spike me.

Coach. Did he try to?

John. No . . . but he looked as if he would.

Doc. *(Disgustedly)* Oh, my God—I don't know whether to put blinders on him or kill him!

Coach. Oh, so you were just scared, is that it?

John. Well . . . I—I just realized that I couldn't possibly beat a man like Hoyt!

Coach. Why not?

John. But he wouldn't let me! That's why I don't want to run in this relay—I'll be worse! I just can't run again.

Coach. Why, is there something the matter with you?

John. I've got the worst thing possible the matter with me——

Magpie. Did you hurt yourself, John?

John. It's worse than that——

Coach. Well, what is it?

John. Oh, I don't like to talk about it.

Doc. "Charley horse"—likely—but get up here and I'll rub it out of you!

John. You can't do that—it's a mental condition.

Magpie. Well, let him rub your head.

Pierce. Shut up, Magpie—who told you all that, John?

John. Somebody who knows. I just found it out yesterday—that's why I never can do anything. *(He drops on table.)*

Coach. What is? Here—come right out with it—no false modesty!

John. *(Reluctantly)* Well—my ego doesn't work right.

Coach. *(After a look at* Magpie*)* Your what?

John. My ego. It's impeded.

Doc. Well, your *legs* are all right, aren't they? After this race is over, you can have your ego operated on.

Coach. Who put this fool notion into your head?

John. Julia Winters—and she knows, too——

COACH. Who's Julia Winters?

PIERCE. That girl from Wisconsin!

COACH. Oh—no wonder! She's trying to make you yellow!

JOHN. No—she's mad at Wisconsin—she wants me to win. *(He shudders.)*

COACH. Do you know her, Magpie?

MAGPIE. Yes—she's up here in the box with Margie Blake.

COACH. Go bring her in here. We've got to get this damn fool idea out of his head before the relay.

MAGPIE. All right—Coach. *(Exit left.)*

JOHN. Don't bring *her* in *here*—— *(Indicates his uncovered legs in embarrassment.)*

COACH. I want to find out about this. "Ego," huh? I don't allow my men to *have* any ego! Get up there and get your legs rubbed. *(JOHN climbs on table.)*

DOC. Take off your shirt! I'll rub that yellow streak off your back. *(JOHN looks resentful.)*

PIERCE. *(Aside to* DOC*)* Don't be mean to him, Doc!

DOC. Well, I got to get after that *ego* trouble! Must be something like *lumbago. (He pronounces it "a-go."* JOHN *stands up, back to audience; removes sweat shirt, showing No. Thirteen* (13) *on his back; sits on table. Starts to pull out* JOHN'S *"gym" shirt from pants)* Take off your shirt!

JOHN. I'd better not undress—if the girls are coming in here!

DOC. *(Pulling his shirt off)* Take it off—you can cover up with the towel. *(*JOHN *grabs towel* PIERCE *is sitting on at* L. *end of table, covers his bare breast as he lies down.* DOC *throws towel up.* JOHN *puts it down.* DOC *puts it up again and eyes* JOHN *severely, as* JOHN *draws his abdomen in, so that he looks very thin indeed.)* You *study* too

much, young fellow. No *wonder* you got "Ego"!

PIERCE. You misunderstood her, John. Why, you're a great runner. *(Turns to* COACH. *Speaks aside)* I believe she can help him, at that. She has great influence with him.

COACH. *(To* PIERCE*)* If she's done any damage, she'd better undo it, that's all. Look here, Miller. You know you're going to run No. Four in the relay team—don't you?

JOHN. *(Sitting up)* No. Four? Why, that's the most important place!

COACH. You bet it is—and we're depending on you to win! Just remember that! Run the way you started out in that four hundred and forty and then keep on running.

JOHN. But I thought I was going to start—just when I'm used to that gun, you go and change me.

COACH. Oh, for God's sake—what makes you so nervous! Look at me—I'm not nervous! *(*JOHN *looks away, frightened.)* Look at me!

JOHN. I saw you.

DOC. Oh—he's all in a cold sweat! Hand me that alcohol, Wallie. *(*PIERCE *hands him bottle labelled "Alcohol."* DOC *claps it on his back.)*

JOHN. *(Shivering at the cold wetness on his bare back)* Ooh! Is that . . . poison?

DOC. No—it's pure grain alcohol—and don't let me catch you drinkin' any, either! You're dizzy enough!

(Enter JULIA *and* MARGIE *from* L.*)*

MARGIE. *(A little embarrassed)* Hello, John— hello, Wallie. *(*JOHN *nods and tries to cover himself with towel. Puts towel over his back, lies down —then finds chest bare and reverses it hastily.)*

JULIA. Oh, this is thrilling—right in with the

athletes! How cute you look, John! (JOHN *moves the towel nervously.*)

COACH. Look here, Miss—*you.* They say you know what's the matter with him.

JULIA. With John? Oh, yes—it's very plain—he has a complex.

COACH. A complex *what?*

JULIA. An inferiority complex.

DOC. Maybe it's in your stomach muscles. *(Feels* JOHN'S *stomach.)*

JULIA. Oh, no—although such neuroses often cause a physical disturbance thereabouts.

COACH. *Where*abouts?

JULIA. In the digestive tract.

DOC. *(Rubbing his stomach)* Feel anything there?

JOHN. *(Pulling the towel down to cover his abdomen)* No!

MARGIE. She means it is just a mental thing in this case, Coach.

COACH. What's that got to do with running, then—this isn't a debating team.

MARGIE. Oh, look, John—you've got a mole on your leg! That's good luck. (JOHN *pulls blanket which covers table up around him.* DOC *puts it down again.* JOHN *then throws towel over legs— suddenly realizes his torso is bare and recovers towel.)*

JOHN. Couldn't you stand over there, you girls? (DOC *pushes him down on table. The girls have placed themselves above table, so that* JOHN *is in constant embarrassment.* MARGIE *now crosses extreme left.)*

JULIA. *(Moving over to* COACH—*lowers her voice)* Why, Coach—I'm surprised to hear you say that a mental state has nothing to do with athletics— after all your experience.

COACH. Oh, I've had plenty of mental states—

but I never had any fellow before come right out and admit that he's a piece of cheese! Now, he's got to run a race in a minute—and you've got him full of this inferiority business. Well—if you're not some kind of a Wisconsin spy or something like that——

MARGIE. Oh, she isn't, Coach—she's rooting for us!

COACH. Well, then—fix him up so he can win—or tell me what's the matter with him.

JULIA. *(Raising her voice a bit)* I can't fix him up so he can win—unless he rises to it *himself!*

COACH. Well, then, for the love of Mike—*rise,* Miller! *(JOHN starts to rise from table. He has been trying to hear.)*

DOC. *(Pushing him down)* Lay down. *(Continues rubbing.)*

JULIA. I tried to key him up—I've given him every incentive to win—*haven't I, Jack? (She stands over him and eyes his bare form.* JOHN *holds towel around him as* DOC *bends both legs over his head so that* JOHN *speaks from an almost inverted position.)*

JOHN. I should say you have! *(JOHN pulls pants to cover legs—then up to cover stomach, finally wraps towel around his waistline desperately.)*

JULIA. After what I told him, he ought to see things from an entirely different point of view.

JOHN. *(Upside down)* Oh, yes, I do.

JULIA. *(Turning to* COACH. *Lowers her voice again)* But it is impossible for an introvert, like John, to respond freely and effectively to external stimuli——

COACH. What did you say he was?

JULIA. An introvert—an emotional introvert.

DOC. *(Catching these last words—holding* JOHN *down, speaks to* COACH*)* I told you there was something wrong with him from the first. An introvert

—for shame! *(Crosses himself in holy horror and begins to wash his hands at table* R.)

MARGIE. Oh . . . that's nothing wrong—that's just the type he belongs to.

JULIA. How do you know?

MARGIE. I read about it in that psychology book last night.

COACH. *(Loudly—getting confusedly angry)* Well —is it *wrong?* We won't stand for any immorality around here!

JULIA. *(Loud)* No—we have no morality in science! *(Doc takes towel from* JOHN *to dry his hands.)*

JOHN. *(Desperately)* *I* have some—give me that towel! *(Grabs towel and covers himself—crouches back of table.)*

MAGPIE. Put his shirt on—he's got to run in a minute! *(*PIERCE *hands him shirt. Goes to door.)*

PIERCE. I'll see how they're coming. *(Exits.* JOHN *puts on shirt, trying to shield himself behind table. Gets head through armhole.)*

JULIA. *(Stepping forward)* Here—I'll help you.

JOHN. *(Frantically)* No! I can do it myself! *(Stoops behind table, tucking shirt in pants.)*

JULIA. *(Turning to* COACH*)* That's a good sign —he tries to do something himself——

MARGIE. Well, he's used to putting his *shirt* on. *(*JOHN *turns away from girls with assumed carelessness; tucks shirt in furiously and turns back.)*

COACH. Why, hell—young lady—if all this stuff is true—— *(*JOHN *down to stool* R.)*

JULIA. It isn't stuff I'm telling you, Mr. Coach— it's *science!*

MARGIE. *(Interrupting with determination; comes to* L. *end of table)* But listen, Julia—you've overlooked something! You know some of those introverts become conquerors, just because they hate to be inferior.

COACH. (L. *of* MARGIE) Conquerors?

MARGIE. Yes . . . in the book it says that sometimes they get so mad at themselves for feeling inferior that they just go after things like a madman—and *nothing* can *stop* them!

COACH. (*Crossing to* JOHN R.) Is that so? Say—didn't you say something like that to Hoyt yesterday, Miller?

JOHN. Oh . . . I was just imagining that.

MARGIE. Well . . . you can imagine it now! Why don't you get a *superiority* complex?

COACH Now you're talking!

JULIA. Oh, that's different—it belongs to another type——

MARGIE. (*Interrupting*) But it amounts to the same thing, Julia. He can do it—if he makes up his mind!

COACH. Well—I thought maybe there was a little common sense some place in all this scientific bunk! I know what he needs—just a good stiff talking to, like I give the men before a football game. You're scared, Miller—just plain scared—and what you need is to get *fighting mad!*

JOHN. No, there's no use in getting me mad—Hoyt can get madder in a minute than I can if I tried all day!

COACH. (*Intensely*) We'll see about that. (*Pulls* JOHN *over; pushes him into camp chair. Sets himself and begins a harangue*) Do you realize that in five minutes you'll be out on that track, that you're the anchor man on our relay team—and that the fate of this meet depends on *you?*

JOHN. There are three *other* fellows on the relay team.

COACH. And they'll all do their duty—it's up to *you!* (*Points his finger at him, and warms to his work*) Not only the meet, but the relay cup—the Gold Cup! You know that—Wisconsin has won it

twice—if they win it again—they keep it! *You* must stop them!

JOHN. *(Cringing)* Couldn't you . . . talk to somebody else now for awhile?

COACH. *(Towering over him)* No . . . I'm talking to you. If we lose it—you're responsible! *You* quit practice last week without permission! *You* dropped the four hundred and forty yard dash when you had it in your pocket! You are going to run *last* for our team! *(JOHN squirms.)* Here's Magpie—he'll be out there leading cheers for *you!* The eyes of *five thousand people* will all be centered right on you—counting your steps, running with you—breathing with you—*winning* with you! And if you don't come through—if you don't *win,* you'll be ashamed ever to show your face again! *(JOHN drops his head in agony.)* You'll be pointed at as the man who was afraid to be spiked! If you ever have any children . . . *(JOHN gives COACH a look of sharp reproval and "hushes" him. Correcting himself)* Or *grand*children—how will they feel when the Gold Cup is mentioned?

MARGIE. They might not mention it.

COACH. Oh, yes—they'd have to say, my father . . . was *afraid* . . . he was full of *mental states*— They would have to say, my father didn't care for his University, or his friends, or his team, or his girl, or his *honor*—or his *Coach!* He was willing to sacrifice us all—because he was afraid of a little thing like being *spiked!*

JOHN. *(Rising in nervous desperation)* Don't say any more! My God,—I'll *win*—if they cut me to pieces! *(He has picked up the folding stool and works it nervously like a bellows.)*

COACH. Ah! . . . Atta boy! *(Steps back.)*

PIERCE. *(Entering)* The high jumps over—they took everything. It's time to call the relay.

COACH. They'll call it. Come on, Doc.

(The locomotive yell is a "locomotive." The "Yea"
is a long drawn out yell, followed by "U, Rah,
Rah!" etc., each syllable sharp and staccato,
slowly at first, then gathering speed in imita-
tion of the start of a locomotive engine.)

CROWD. *(In cellar)*
Yea! ! !
U, Rah, Rah, Wis — con — sin
U, Rah, Rah, Wis — con — sin
U, Rah, Rah, Wis — con — sin.
Yea——! ! Yea——! ! ! Yeah——! ! !
On, Wisconsin, on, Wisconsin, fight on for your
fame,
Run the bal—etc. *(As before, repeat chorus, singing*
two choruses altogether, followed by the locomotive.
Giving altogether at this point and in that order:

  1 *locomotive (as above).*
  2 *choruses, "On Wisconsin."*
  1 *locomotive.*

DOC. All right . . . don't forget what you said,
young fellow.

JOHN. *(Looking at* MARGIE*)* All right, I'm
ready. (Doc *exits left.)*

JULIA. *(Coming up to him)* That's the old Spar-
tan spirit, John.

JOHN. *(Crossing* C. *to her desperately)* Oh,
Julia . . . you know what you said last night.

JULIA. Yes . . . and I meant it—if you beat
Spike!

JOHN. *(Hopefully)* Oh . . . I'm not going to
hold you to that, Julia——

JULIA. *(Sternly)* I mean it. *(Goes to flap of*
tent) And you must win! Come back *with* your
shield—or *on it,* Jack! *(She exits.)*

PIERCE. *(Tensely, going over to him, slaps his*
shoulder) Come on, John. *(Exits.)*

(COACH *eyes* JOHN, *makes a vigorous gesture of
punching one fist into other palm, and follows.*
MARGIE *stands watching* JOHN, *whose face is
tragic as he imitates the coach's punching gesture. Suddenly he stretches out in agony, and
drops on the trainer's table—sobbing and laughing hysterically.*)

MARGIE. *(Putting her hand on his shoulder)*
John . . .

JOHN. *(Sobbing)* Oh, what am I going to do?
What am I going to *do?*

MARGIE. Oh, what am *I* going to do? (MARGIE
*looks around, worried; sees glass of water on table;
picks it up. Her eye catches the alcohol; she takes
it—smells it, puts her tongue to it, and pours a little
into the water)* Here, John—pull yourself together!
(He sits up, still shaking.) Here, drink this! *(He
takes glass, drinks it, chokes a bit.)*

JOHN. Oh—what is that?

MARGIE. It won't hurt you—it's just some—aro-
matic spirits of ammonia. Now, John—you mustn't
break down like this. I thought you were going to
win!

JOHN. Oh, I don't know what to do!

MARGIE. Well . . . if you can't—perhaps it's
wrong to make you try so hard. I'm not going to
urge you to. I don't think it's right to make it a
matter of life and death——

JOHN. *(Brokenly)* Oh, but it is!

MARGIE. No, it isn't. The world isn't going to
come to an end . . . and people will soon forget about
it, no matter what you do!

JOHN. Oh, no, they won't.

MARGIE. Yes, they will. Why, I'd like you just
as well if you never won anything.

JOHN. You would?

MARGIE. *(Soothing him)* Of course—— Now don't be so frightened.

JOHN. I'm not frightened—of Hoyt—I've made up my mind to that now—I don't care if he does murder me now——

MARGIE. Well, then, what's the matter?

JOHN. I don't *know!* I just feel as if I *can't* run that race. I know I've got to—they're all counting on me—the fellows, and the coach—and Julia—do you know what she said to me last night? *(Turns to her suddenly.)*

MARGIE. What?

JOHN. She told me if I beat Spike—she'd *marry* me!

MARGIE. Well, that ought to be enough to make you win.

JOHN. Yes ... it ought to ... I can't understand why I feel—this way—I just feel—*paralyzed!*

MARGIE. *(Looking at him questioningly)* John ... you do love Julia—don't you?

(WARN Curtain.)

JOHN. *(Startled)* What?

MARGIE. I say you do love Julia—don't you?

JOHN. *(With the earnestness of the unsure)* Why, yes—of *course* I love her—only——

MARGIE. Only what?

JOHN. She makes me so darn *nervous!* Oh, I didn't mean that—— *(Paces up and down—stops L. of table)* That's funny, isn't it? For a fellow like me to not be sure he loves a wonderful girl like Julia! Of course I love her! I love her ... something *terrible. (Crosses down R.)* And I've *got* to win now for her—she's going to *marry* me if I *win*—— Oh, my God! *(He suddenly breaks again and drops sobbing on the camp stool R.)*

MARGIE. *(Comes over to him swiftly, like a mother to a hurt child, pats him, puts her arm around*

him) Don't, John—don't! Come on now—buck up, old man!

JOHN.   I can't!—I can't!   *(She leans over and lifts his head, and kisses him, slowly. He suddenly quiets, rises slowly and looks at her strangely. Speaks with terrific gravity)* You don't know what that did for me—I feel *all* right now.   *Off Stage Call, "Places For The Relay!"*

MARGIE.   Are you sure?

JOHN.   Yes . . . *wonderful ! !* Excuse me, won't you . . . but just for a minute it came over me as if . . . if I didn't love Julia—but I love her now! I can *feel* it!

MARGIE.   Of course you do——

JOHN.   I never felt like this before—as if I was on wings—or something.   *(Rises on tiptoe; extends arms like a Sandow.)*

(Offstage the ANNOUNCER *calls: "Place for the Relay. Last call."* JOHN *starts.)*

MARGIE.   *(Putting her hand on his shoulder)* You're going to win now—for her!

JOHN.   *(Holding* MARGIE'S *hand in passionate resolve)* Oh, yes, my dear—that's *right*, for her—— Sure!

(Offstage the megaphone—"Places for the Relay— Last call!"

(He straightens up, relinquishes her hands, and goes to battle—a consecrated knight.

(As he breaks into a dog trot through the flap of the tent, MARGIE *watches him tenderly.)*

THE CURTAIN FALLS

*(As curtain falls we hear the crowd singing "Car-
men Ohio"; the song continues until curtain
rises on Scene II.)*

SCENE II

SCENE II: *The track in front of the Boxes, in a corner of the Stadium.*

The front part of the stage is the cinder track, running across R. to L. The start and finish line is dead center. Above the track a narrow strip of grass with a bench right and one on left for the competing athletes. Between these benches steps lead up the raised platform of the boxes, which is backed by a solid wall, with trees and sky behind. In the box R. of center we see what seems to be the party of the President of the University. The other boxes (there are four in all) are filled with students and faculty members. A railing runs off R. and L. above the track, with rooters crowded behind it on each side of the stage. Red and grey bunting and Ohio State pennants on railings.

AT RISE: MARGIE *and* JULIA *are discovered in box, left of center. Other members of the cast and extras are in the other boxes.* MAGPIE *is in the little quadrangle R., where he leads cheers. Two Wisconsin runners are seated on the bench in the quadrangle left, tightening their shoelaces, etc.* MAGPIE *is leading the song, "Carmen Ohio," which ends as curtain rises. Crowd standing, hats in hands, sits at end of song.* MAGPIE *is dressed in white flannel trousers and white shirt and sweater.*

(Song: "Carmen Ohio." Tune, "Spanish Chant.")

72

Oh, come let's sing Ohio's praise
And songs to Alma Mater raise
While our hearts rebounding thrill
With joy which death alone can still,
Summers' heat and winters' cold,
The seasons pass, the years will roll,
Time and change will surely show
How firm our friendship's, O-hi-O.

*(This song can be started immediately on drop of
curtain at finish of "tent scene," giving ample
time to "strike" tent, etc., and curtain can be
raised on last word of song O-hi-O.)*

(The CROW *applauds and whistles as* MAGPIE *"talks
it up.")*

MAGPIE. *(Leading cheer)* All right, now, bunch.
Let's give them an all "O-hio"—— Ready—hip—
hip——

CROW.   O—O—O—O—
            H—H—H—H—
            I—I—I—I—
            O—O—O—O—
            OHIO!

(Off stage R. *the* ANNOUNCER *is heard calling
through his megaphone.)*

ANNOUNCER. "The next and last event is the
one-mile relay race. The score in this dual meet
now stands: Wisconsin, 68—Ohio State, 64. The
team winning the relay scores five points—

MAGPIE. *(Seizing his megaphone, addresses the
crowd)* Did you hear that—Wisconsin, 68—Ohio
State, 64—— If we get this relay, we win the meet!
The Gold Cup depends on this race! Come on, now
—let's give 'em a locomotive! Ready! *(He leads
with extravagant gestures the cheer.)*

THE CROWD. *(Very slowly)*
Rah . . . rah . . . rah . . . Ohio State, Ohio State!
      (Slightly faster)
Rah, rah, rah, rah, Ohio State, Ohio State!
      (Faster)
Rah-rah-rah-rah—Ohio State—Ohio State!
      (Very fast and loud)
Rah-rah-rah-rah—Ohio State—Ohio State!
      (Then, as MAGPIE *leaps, the crowd rises, with a
      whistle)*
Wheeeeeeeeeeeeeeeeeeeeee! BOOM, OHIO!

*(*MAGPIE *turns a handspring on "Boom." Crowd
      sits again.*
*(The two Wisconsin runners begin to jog up and
      down, lifting their knees high, warming up.*
*(Two Ohio State runners appear from right and be-
      gin to warm up; they are greeted by scattered
      cheers.*
*(*HOYT *and the fourth Wisconsin runner appear
      from left and begin to warm up.* HOYT *prances
      up in front of the boxes.)*

MARGIE. *(Pointing for* JULIA's *benefit)* There's
Spike Hoyt!
JULIA. I see him. *(She pretends not to notice
him as he looks at her. As he turns and repasses she
says)* Oh—— Hello, Spike!
HOYT. *(Sore)* Hello yourself. *(Prances on
past and off* L.)

*(*COACH JACKSON, *accompanied by* DOC, HUB
      SMITH *and the* OFFICIAL STARTER, *appear from
      R. and take place center.* PROFESSOR DEMING,
      *with "Official" ribbon pinned on lapel, is in box
      R.C.* HUB *and* SMITH *have stop-watches.*
      PROFESSOR *carries the "tape" for finish.* START-
      ER *has revolver.)*

COACH. *(To the* STARTER*)* All right, Mr. Stone
—get them started. Where's Pierce and Miller?

DOC. Don't ask me. (PIERCE *appears from right,
and is greeted by cheers. He begins to warm up.*)

MAGPIE. *(Shouting)* Knock 'em dead—Wallie!

STARTER. All right, you fellows—get your places!

(The seven men gather left of center. PIERCE *begins
to dig his holes, on downstage side of track.*)

HOYT. Hey—wait a minute—— Who gave you
the pole?

STARTER. *(Spins a coin)* Toss for it.

PIERCE. Call it, Hoyt!

HOYT. Heads!

STARTER. It's tails.

HOYT. All right—go ahead. (PIERCE *smiles and
resumes digging. This is done with foot, the spikes
digging a transverse trench. Other five men move
extreme left, "loosening up."*)

PIERCE. *(Looking around)* Whe·e's Miller?

DOC. *(Looking around)* Ain't he here?

(JOHN *enters from right, striding high. He bumps
into the* COACH, *as* COACH *has back turned,
explaining something to Wisconsin Official.*
COACH *gives him an impatient push that almost
upsets him.*)

COACH. Hey—they're waiting for you! *(Turns.)*

JOHN. Oh, excuse me!

STARTER. Get down here—you!

JOHN. Well, I've got to warm up. *(Prances a
bit off* R. *and returns, stepping high.*)

COACH. Bring your knees up! (JOHN *prances,
knees almost to his chin.*)

JULIA. *(Leaning over rail, waves her kerchief in
his face)* Hello, John! (JOHN *shies away and*

*bends his head so that he hits himself in chin; holds
his chin. The crowd laughs.)* Aren't you going to
speak to me?

JOHN. I bit my tongue!

STARTER. Hey—get over here!

JOHN. Certainly—I didn't know you were ready.
(JOHN *moves over to lower side of track at start
line.* HOYT *begins to dig holes and kick cinders over*
JOHN, *getting one in his eye.)* Hey, you're getting
them in my eyes!

HOYT. Well, are you too lazy to blink? *(Continues digging.)*

DOC. That starting line don't look straight to me.
(Goes to upstage side, stoops and squints. HOYT
gives JOHN *a final faceful and steps back.* JOHN,
not seeing DOC, *turns back and begins kicking cinders at* HOYT; *they hit* DOC *in the face.)* Hey, what
the hell are you doing!

JOHN. *(In confusion)* Oh, I didn't know it was
you! I'm digging a hole. (DOC *walks over and
looks at him severely, examines hole.)*

HOYT. *(Laughing scornfully—stepping in front
of box; addresses* JULIA*)* That bird will get plenty
of cinders kicked in his face when he runs against
me.

MARGIE. You'll have to be in front to do that.

HOYT. I'll be in front, all right—don't worry!
(Turns to JULIA*)* I suppose you're rooting for him,
eh? Well, you saw what I did to him in the four
forty, didn't you?

DOC. *(To* JOHN*)* And you don't need any holes
—*you're* not starting—Pierce is!

JOHN. Oh—that's right. *(Moves over to box)*
It's too bad I won't get to run against Mr. Hoyt
again. Pierce is running first.

HOYT. What's that? Hey—wait a minute!

STARTER. You're starting for your team, aren't
you, Hoyt?

HOYT. Just a minute! Where is this bird running?

JULIA. Jack is running last—in the place of honor, and what's that got to do with you, Mr. Hoyt?

HOYT. It's got a whole lot to do with me. Wait, Starter. I'm going to change the order of our team.

STARTER. What's that?

JOHN. *(Anxiously)* Oh, that's all right—I'm satisfied—even if I *don't* get a chance to beat you.

HOYT. I wouldn't rob you of that pleasure. Here, Starter—Simms will run first, and I'm last! *(He whispers in ear of SIMMS, his team-mate.)*

STARTER. Well, any way—but make up your mind. (SIMMS *takes place at starting line; measures his holes.* PIERCE *does likewise below him.)*

JOHN. *(Coming over hastily)* Maybe I *had* better run *first!*

COACH. *(Shouting)* Oh, shut up! Get them started, Mr. Stone. (PROFESSOR, *down from box, stands with* HUB *up* C.)

STARTER. *(Placing himself behind the start line— i.e., left of it)* Now, you men understand, you got ten yards each side—— *(Points off* R.) to transfer the baton. *(He hands a polished stick to* PIERCE *and* SIMMS. JOHN *stands in middle of track, looking at stick in deathly fascination.)* Hey—don't stand on the track, Miller—get to one side—you're number four! Now you fellers get in order, at each side. Number two—number three—number four— like that; then as you see your men coming with the stick—— *(He points off* L.) Don't run back of that line to meet him—or you're disqualified.

(Ohio men in file downstage, Wisconsin above.)

HOYT. Oh, we know all that!

STARTER. Well, don't forget it! Do *you* understand, Miller?

JOHN. *(R.C.)* Yes, but—you can start to run, can't you?

COACH. *(Stepping up R. of JOHN)* Sure, start to run—as your man gets close to the finish—but remember he has to give you the baton between these two lines! *(Points to line L. of start and to line off R.)*

JOHN. But that's only ten yards each side—— He might not catch up to me.

PIERCE. Oh, he'll—*(Pointing to Ohio's number three man)*—catch up to you, all right. Don't be so nervous, John.

JOHN. I'm not nervous—I'm just afraid I might run too *fast*.

HOYT. *(Nudging SIMMS)* Did you hear that one?—he's afraid he'll run too *fast!* He ought to have brakes on! *(Grins at JULIA.)*

COACH. Just be sure that you've got a good hold on the baton—before the other fellow lets go of it!

JOHN. That's the trouble—that stick looks slippery!

DOC. *(Viciously)* What!

JOHN. I'm afraid I might drop it!

HOYT. Give him some rubber gloves.

DOC. If you drop it you'll never live to drop another one!

JOHN. I know it—but that's no comfort to me. *(DOC makes a "pass" at him. JOHN crosses below runners to L.)*

COACH. All right,—places! Ready, Mr. Stone? *(The OFFICIAL nods. HUB and PROFESSOR begin to stretch tape.)* Here, wait a minute—— Don't put the tape up until the last two men have started—just for the last lap.

JOHN. And hold it up high—so I won't trip over it *(HOYT glares at him.)*

STARTER *and* DOC. Shut up!

(JOHN *retires to bench up* L. *with other runners.*
HUB *drops back up center with* PROFESSOR.)

STARTER. All right, men—— On your marks!
(PIERCE *and* SIMMS *crouch at the start. The other
runners and the crowd lean forward tensely.*) Get
set! (*Both men rise in a tense grouch. Just an instant before the gun,* SIMMS *starts and both "break,"
beating the gun.* STARTER *immediately fires a second shot, recalling them. The two men jog back, a
trifle shamefaced.*) Here, come back here. What's
the matter with you? You both broke—so I won't
penalize you—but remember if I catch either one of
you this next time—it's two yards back you'll start.

JOHN. (*Trembling with excitement*) Good Lord,
I'm glad that wasn't me!

(STARTER, DOC, COACH *and others join in "Shut
up!"*)

STARTER. Shut up!—Now—on your marks——
(*They crouch.*) Get set—— (*Same business.*)

DOC. Bang! (*As the gun is fired both men are
off and disappear off* R. PIERCE *gets a slight lead
on the jump.*)

MARGIE. (*Shouting as she watches off* R.) Wallie's ahead—— Look at him go around that curve—

MAGPIE. (*Addressing crowd*) Come on, now—
A Pierce rah—quick!——

THE CROWD. Pierce Rah—Pierce Rah—Rah—
rah—*Pierce!*

MAGPIE. (*Pointing straight out front*)   C
Look at him go—he's got five yards on   O
him! (MAGPIE *points out runners' pro-*   N
gress. Crowd follows him.)   S

JULIA. What do you think of that,   T
Spike?   A

SPIKE. Oh, Pierce is their *best man*—   N
wait till we get started!   T

JOHN. *(Jumping out on track beside the waiting Wisconsin No. Two)* Oh, Lord, I hope I don't drop that stick.

DOC. *(Pushing him)* Get back—it isn't your next—you damn fool—it's him! *(Pulls Ohio No. Two out.)*

MARGIE. *(Pointing off L.)* Here they come!

MAGPIE. *(Screaming)* Come on, Pierce—hold that lead! Hold that lead!

THE CROWD. Come on, Wallie—that a-boy, Pierce—hold that lead—keep coming, etc., etc.

(PIERCE dashes on as No. Two starts. They transfer stick and No. Two is off to a flying start.

(A moment behind comes SIMMS and the second Wisconsin man is off on the trail.)

Ad Lib.
FROM CROWD
Excitement and Constant Yells From Crowd. On Its Feet.

HOYT. *(Yelling)* Go get him, Mark—he's easy! Get ready, Kid—Marky will give you a lead! *(He slaps Wisconsin No. Three, who edges out on track.)*

(HUB throws a blanket around PIERCE, who has dropped on the Ohio bench.)

MARGIE. *(Leaning over)* Good work, Wallie! *(He smiles.)* Oh, look——— *(MAGPIE shouts. MARGIE points front)* Wisconsin is catching up to us!

(PIERCE rises and watches anxiously.)

MAGPIE. *(Pointing front)* He's passing! *(Turns upstage, hands to his head.)*

(Cue to CROWD.)

Crowd Groans and Shows That Wisconsin Is Ahead.

THE WISCONSIN RUNNER: Yea—Marky—Yeah—Marky! Go to it, boy, etc., etc.

PIERCE. Pete is hanging right with him!

HOYT. *(Excitedly—points to left curve)* That's the kid, Marky—— *(Slaps No. Three)* He's got a *lead!*

JOHN. Maybe he'll slip!

HOYT. *(Coaching No. Three Wisconsin)* Ready, now—Kid—here he comes! *(The Wisconsin and Ohio Nos. Three are ready at the line.)* All right—start. *(Wisconsin No. Three starts as No. Two dashes in and he is off.)*

Nearly Everyone Sits Down.

Crowd Still Discouraged As Wisconsin Comes In Five Yards Ahead.

(Very close behind, Ohio No. Two transfers stick and No. Three is off. Crowd cheers as JONES starts fast.)

MAGPIE. Come on, Jonesie—catch him! Look at that boy run. He's right on his heels.

THE CROWD. Come on, Jones—pass him—go around him—etc., etc.

DOC. *(Sharply)* You're next, Miller!

HOYT. *(Getting ready himself)* I'll say he's next!

EXCITEMENT

(JOHN looks nervous and runs up and down.)

MAGPIE. *(Leaps in air)* Look at that! *(Points across the field.* CROWD *cheers spontaneously.)*

Grows As JONES Gains. Crowd To Feet

MARGIE. *(Pounding* JULIA*)* Look —Jonesie's ahead of him!

PIERCE. He's gaining every step! He'll give you a good lead, John.

JOHN. I'll need it, all right. *(Begins to nervously run left.)*

DOC. Hey—don't cross that line! (JOHN *jumps back as from hot metal.)*

MARGIE. Good luck, John!

JULIA. *(Sharply)* Run—Jack! Here he comes!

(JOHN *nervously starts to run ahead right.)*

PIERCE *and* MAGPIE. Wait!

COACH. *(Pushing him back)* Get back, there—you've got a ten yard lead! *Now!*

(JOHN *retreats left—sees* JONES; *starts* R. JONES *dashes on, and as* JOHN *tries too nervously to grab the stick—he drops it.)*

(There is a wail from the crowd, as he scrambles for it.

(Meanwhile HOYT *has waited surely for his man and gets a flying start. Just as* JOHN *finally grabs the stick from the ground,* HOYT *darts past.)*

JOHN. *(As he scrambles)* Oh, God help me—— *(He recovers it and is off on* HOYT'S *heels.)*

DOC. Kill him, Coach—you're closer to him!

MARGIE. *(Screaming)* Run, John!

JULIA. Oh, the idiot—what made him drop it!

DOC. I knew he'd do it——

COACH. The damn fool—he'll never catch Hoyt now!

THE CROWD. *(Muttering)* The poor sap—wouldn't you know he'd do that—losing that big lead—run, you oilcan—run! etc.

PIERCE. *(Pointing front)* He's sticking with him! Hoyt isn't gaining any more.

MAGPIE. But he'll never catch him! *(Begins to tear his shirt off.)*

MARGIE. Yes, he will! Yes, he will! Why don't you *cheer!*

THE WISCONIN RUNNERS. Come on, Hoyt—that-a-boy! Keep going!—yeah, *Hoyt!*

MAGPIE. My God—Miller's caught up to him! *(Leaps in air. Cue to* CROWD.*)*

PIERCE. *(Looking off* L. *curve)* You can't tell on the curve.

MAGPIE. Yes, he has—come on, Miller!

MARGIE. *(Leading the crowd)* Come on, Miller—come on, Miller!

COACH. They can't hold that pace! Stretch that tape—Prof., here they come!

(The PROFESSOR *and* HUB *tighten the tape across finish line.)*

MAGPIE. They're abreast! Come

AND REPROACHES FROM CROWD

From Here On The Wildest Growing Excitement And Hectic Shouting— Yells, Pleading, Etc.

on, Miller! *(Leaps onto* Pierce's *shoulders.)*

All the Wisconsin Runners. Come on, *Hoyt!*

All the Ohio Rooters. Come on, Miller! !

Doc. They're falling down—they're cracking—— Come on, Miller!

(The two runners, so exhausted that their pace has slowed a bit, burst into view, John *one yard ahead.* John *leaps ahead, lunges and breaks tape. They fall and roll over the finish together. In doing so* John's *foot strikes* Hoyt's *hip. The crowd drops to excited chatter, uncertain of result.*

(The three Wisconsin runners rush out to Hoyt, *cover him with blanket and carry him right with cheers.)*

W
I
L
D
E
S
T

Y
E
L
L
S

O
F

A
L
L

Wisconsin Runners. Attaboy, Spike—I think you got it!

Hoyt. Ouch—my leg! He spiked me!

Julia. *(Running to* Hoyt) Oh, Spike—you were wonderful!

Margie. *(Who has run down to* John, *raising him up from his prostrate position* r.c.) Oh, John—I thought *you* won! *(*John, *a little groggy—looks up, gasping.)*

Pierce. *(Excitedly to Officials who are grouped down* l., *conferring)* Well, who wins? *(Crowd hushes to listen.)*

Starter. *(Shouts decision)* Ohio State *wins!*

Margie. Listen, John—you did win!

(JOHN *smiles happily, tries to rise.*
MAGPIE, HUB *and* PIERCE *dash up
to* JOHN; *others follow, grouping
right—athletes,* COACH, DOC, PRO-
FESSOR, *etc.* CROWD *yells wildly
as they pick him up.*)

HUB *and* PIERCE. *(Shout, as they
and* MAGPIE *pull* JOHN *to his feet)*
You won the race, John, old kid—*you
won!*

(MAGPIE, *excited, addresses Crowd.*)

MAGPIE. Come on, gang! *(They
hush to hear him as he holds up
hands.)*

(As crowd hushes slightly and JOHN
looks around happily JULIA *rushes
to* R.C. *and stops dramatically.*)

*(These two lines must be heard. All cheering
stopped.)*

JULIA. John—you *won!* Oh, my *dear!*
JOHN. *(Collapsing as he sees* JULIA *is upon him)*
Oh, my God!

*(The boys catch him and fan him—as
Crowd cheers.)*

CURTAIN

*C
H
E
E
R
I
N
G*

*C
H
E
E
R
I
N
G*

*H
U
S
H*

*Loud
Cheer
As
Curtain
Falls.*

ACT III

SCENE: *The living room of the Psi Sigma House. A good looking room in dark oak wainscoting and beams, decorated for a dance.*

Double doors up center show a hall running off right and left. A sofa is seen in this hall. A French window, right, opens upon a porch, which is dimly seen. Up L., on a table against the wall, are plates of sandwiches, a grand piano down R., with a sofa against the wall up R. A sofa L.C., backed by a narrow table with a pretty lamp, a fireplace L. with a picture above it of a gentleman of the 1850 period, the founder of the fraternity. Silver and bronze cups on the mantle, a bronze plaque or two over the mantle and another on the wall of the hall. Several large square banners on the walls above the wainscoting: Ohio State, Wisconsin, Illinois, etc. (No small triangular pennants.)

AT RISE: *Group around piano R. One boy is playing jazz. There is a group scattered about the stage, eating sandwiches, drinking punch and chattering. Some are talking about the result of the track meet, congratulating WALLIE PIERCE, remarking on JACK MILLER'S surprising achievement, etc. Another group, consisting of HUB and BETTY, are up L. of the C. door. They are talking about BETTY'S dress, a subject which she finds very interesting. REGGIE is*

86

Act III, "The Poor Nut"

also in this group. Another group with HELEN, *another* GIRL *and two of the Ohio runners, down* R., *about the piano.* MARGIE *is seated on the sofa down* L. *quietly with* PROFESSOR DEMING.

As the dance music starts, the FRESHMAN *enters from up* C. *and goes to* REGGIE.

FRESHMAN. Reggie, can I have this dance?

REGGIE. No, I'm sorry. *(Goes to* HELEN R.*)*

FRESHMAN. Helen, may I have this dance?

HELEN. I'll let you have the eighteenth.

FRESHMAN. Thank you. *(Goes to* BETTY *up* L.C.*)* Betty, may I have this dance?

BETTY. Why, no. I'm sorry, Norry, but it's taken.

FRESHMAN. May I have the next one?

BETTY. Oh, all right, the next one. *(Goes to* MARGIE.*)*

(Music starts—off L.—*Phonograph record, "All Alone," Victor record No.* 19505a. *Repeat record until cue.* PROFESSOR: *"Rather windy, wasn't it?" Others troop out to dance.)*

FRESHMAN. *(To* MARGIE*)* Can I have this dance?

MARGIE. I'm a little tired.

FRESHMAN. You haven't danced much this evening.

MARGIE. That's why.

PROFESSOR. Miss Blake is going to sit out this dance with me.

FRESHMAN. It's funny, but ever since the first dance, I haven't been able to *get* any.

PROFESSOR. *(Smiling)* Help yourself to some sandwiches, Norton.

FRESHMAN. I've had a lot of them. They're good. If I get this dance in, maybe I'll be able to eat some more. *(Exits, grabbing a sandwich as he goes up* C. *Music offstage and all troop out but* MARGIE *and* PROFESSOR.*)*

MARGIE. I'm afraid I'm not very entertaining, Professor.

PROFESSOR. I've been thinking of what you told me. You say Julia really promised John that if he won that race she would marry him?

MARGIE. *(Worried)* That's what he told me.

PROFESSOR. It seems ridiculous, though, doesn't it?

MARGIE. Well . . . Julia is just the kind of girl John needs, I guess. She'll make a big man of him. And Mr. Deming—don't you think John *needs* someone to spur him on—make him do things?

PROFESSOR. *(Thoughtfully, with a touch of sarcasm)* No, I don't think so, but then, perhaps I'm prejudiced. You see, I happened to get a wife who just let me do the things I liked to do . . . Unfortunate, no doubt.

MARGIE. Well . . . *You* came out all right.

PROFESSOR. Yes . . . but we had some pretty hard times—my wife had to go through some lean years with me An old-fashioned custom, my dear.

MARGIE. Oh . . . I'll bet *she* didn't mind!

PROFESSOR. No . . . I don't believe she did . . . I don't like to see John take this step—without thought . . .

MARGIE. *(Quickly)* If he *thought,* he wouldn't take it—I mean——

PROFESSOR. *(Thinking)* Of course one should not interfere—— *(She shakes her head.* PROFESSOR *does likewise.)*

MARGIE. *(Worried)* It wouldn't be loyal to Julia, would it?

PROFESSOR. Well, that is a matter of—meta-

physics . . . But a man should make these decis-
ions *for himself*.

MARGIE. Oh, of course— *(Nods—he imitates)*
but it's so hard to get John to decide *right!*

PROFESSOR. *(Smiling wisely)* I think, my dear,
that perhaps you could—I wouldn't say "indicate"
to John——

MARGIE. Oh, I wouldn't *indicate*—— *(Shakes
head "no."* PROFESSOR *imitates gravely.)*

PROFESSOR. But you might perhaps—well—*precipitate* . . .

MARGIE. Well—maybe I could do that—I wouldn't
do a thing to interfere with John's—I mean with
their happiness . . . but there's one thing I do hate
to see John give up!

PROFESSOR. *(Sympathetically)* What's that, my
dear?

MARGIE. His Algae.

PROFESSOR. What?

MARGIE. He was telling me about his collection
of Algae. He says they're the most important things
in the whole world! What are Algae?

PROFESSOR. Well, have you ever noticed the scum
on ponds?

MARGIE. Yes——

PROFESSOR. Well—that's Algae.

MARGIE. *(Disappointed)* Oh—is that all?

PROFESSOR. But they are important. If there
were no Algae there would be no fish—and what a
dreadful world this would be—without fish! (BETTY
*and one of the Ohio runners tiptoe in, making for
the porch.* PROFESSOR *and* MARGIE *are turned left
silently.* PROFESSOR *hears them, and as they get* R.C.,
speaks without turning) Good evening!

BOY. *(Embarrassed)* Oh—*good evening!* (Gets
to door R.)

BETTY. *(Startled)* Oh, good evening, Professor! *(Follows* BOY *out; speaks as she exits)* How

the Hell did he know we were in here? *(Disappears.)*

PROFESSOR. Margie, I wonder if it's really the Algae that you're worried about.

MARGIE. *(Hesitates)* Well . . . I want him to be happy. *(Drops her head.)*

PROFESSOR. So do I . . . but I'm not quite sure what to do about it. John has always wanted to be like those other boys—he has been unhappy because he was not—shall we say, *standardized?*

MARGIE. *(With a tiny sniffle)* You mean, like a Ford?

PROFESSOR. Exactly. All these boys he admires are standardized—they think alike, they look alike; they become bond salesmen, or real estate men. Of course, in my day it was different. But don't you worry about it. I daresay Julia was only joking about marrying him.

MARGIE. *(Hopefully)* Oh, do you think so?

PROFESSOR. *(Encouragingly)* Yes—and if she wasn't she'll think better of it. College romances usually . . . don't happen.

MARGIE. *(Brightening up)* Well . . . you've made me feel a lot better.

PROFESSOR. *(Rises, crosses L. of sofa. In tones of a conspirator)* And if anything does happen— you and I will have to er . . . *precipitate* something. Now—— *(Music ends.* BETTY *and* BOY *enter from porch. Her hair is mussed up.* PROFESSOR, *smiling wisely)* Been cooling off?

BETTY. Yes, we've been enjoying the fresh air—

PROFESSOR. *(Looking at her hair)* Rather windy, wasn't it?

(Stop Dance Music.)

BETTY. Huh? Oh—— *(Begins to smooth her hair as* BOY *nervously begins to play jazz at piano.)*

(Others enter from up center. Enter chattering,
HELEN *and* FRESHMAN, HUB, REGGIE *and*
PIERCE *and others.* MAGPIE *enters from* R.,
removes flannel case and holds aloft the gold
cup, standing center.)

MAGPIE. Here, bunch! Rub your eyes and look
at this!

MARGIE. *(Crosses to* MAGPIE*)* Oh, the Gold
Cup—isn't it beautiful?

PIERCE. How did you get it up here, Magpie?

MAGPIE. They just brought it from the engravers.
(All look and exclaim.) I'll take it over to the gym
in the morning.

HUB. We had the names of the relay team en-
graved on it.

MARGIE. Oh, then John's name is on it?

MAGPIE. Put it on the piano, Margie. *(She does*
so.)

MARGIE. Oh, this is quite an honor! *(Simul-*
taneously FRESHMAN *and* BETTY *separate from the*
crowd and move left toward punch bowl.)

MAGPIE. *(To* HUB. *Points at* BETTY*)* She's a
peach, isn't she?

HUB. Oh, she's with Norrie—let him alone.

MAGPIE. That *freshman*——! No—I've got to
have her. *(Who has his eye on* BETTY*)* The next
dance is mine, isn't it, Betty?

BETTY. *(As the* FRESHMAN *shakes his head at*
her*)* Why, no. I'm sorry, but it's Norrie's. *(Door-*
bell off right.)

MAGPIE. *(With upperclass authority)* Answer
the door, Fresh.

FRESHMAN. Aw, say, listen——

MAGPIE. You heard me, Little Nemo! *(*FRESH-
MAN *exits* R. *sulkily, after pantomiming protest to*
MAGPIE *without result.)*

BETTY. *(Making the best of it)* Aren't freshmen funny? *(Smiles encouragement at* MAGPIE *and tastes punch.* PIERCE *joins* HUB L.*)*

REGGIE. *(From near piano)* "Freshman"—what do you think *you* are, Betty?

MAGPIE. Now don't be catty.

BETTY. Oh, there's no punch in this punch!

MAGPIE. *(Loudly)* What do you think we are, a bunch of drunkards? *(Then quietly, showing her flask in his pocket)* Come out on the porch and I'll fix you up.

BETTY. Oh, I'd just love to see the moon. *(They exit right to porch, gaily.* FRESHMAN *enters from up center.)*

FRESHMAN. Where's Betty?

HUB. She went out with Magpie to enjoy the moonshine.

FRESHMAN. Oh, I wish Magpie would get a girl of his own. *(Exits glumly to porch.)*

REGGIE. Say, where is this Miller boy, Wallie—I want to meet him.

PIERCE. I left him upstairs, dolling up in Hub's coat and Magpie's white flannels.

(MUSIC Starts.)

REGGIE. Oh, I thought he was with Julia Winters.

*(*HOYT *enters, walking lame. Looks at the bunch sulkily.)*

PROFESSOR. Come in, Brother Hoyt. *(Shakes hands, using fraternity "grip.")*

REGGIE *and* HUB. Good evening.

PIERCE. Hello, Hoyt.

HOYT. Hello yourself.

PROFESSOR. I'm glad you're here. I had a hard time inducing Hoyt to come.

HOYT. I had a hard time to walk. But I won't stay long. I'm getting out on the twelve-thirty.

HUB. What's the matter, are you sore, Hoyt?

HOYT. Say, who wouldn't be sore, after the deal I got this afternoon.

(MARGIE *exits disdainfully* R. *and immediately afterward* MAGPIE *and* BETTY *enter from porch.*)

PROFESSOR. I'm sorry you feel that way, Mr. Hoyt—but your own coach agreed. He said he had warned you about John.

HOYT. *(Feeling leg painfully)* He didn't warn me that this bird Miller was a mowing machine. You ought to see my leg where it's spiked.

JULIA. *(Entering center in time to hear last line)* Really, Mr. Hoyt? Well, you're the one who put this spiking idea into John's head.

HOYT. *(Turning)* That's right—stick up for that murderer!

MAGPIE. *(Winking at* JULIA*)* Why, Julia—that isn't showing the right feeling for your fiance! *(The group giggles.)*

JULIA. *(To* MAGPIE*) Fiance——* Doesn't it occur to you that that is a title to which he has lost the right—*(To* HUB*)*—through his own choice?

HOYT. What do you mean?

(FRESHMAN *and* BETTY *on piano bench.*)

JULIA. You know what I mean—you big dumbbell! *(As others giggle,* JULIA *approaches him and hisses in a whisper)* Didn't you break off our engagement yesterday, right in front of everybody?

HOYT. *(Aloud, in his excitement)* Oh, you ought to have known I didn't mean that. I was mad.

JULIA. I suppose you didn't mean what you said

about Jack, either—that he couldn't run. Well, I
want you to know that I made him beat you today.

MAGPIE. *(Sings)* She made him what he is today! Oh—did that come out of *me?*

JULIA. Yes, and I can make him anything I want
to—he doesn't sneer at my psychoanalysis in the
ignorant way you do! *(Turns R.)*

HOYT. Oh, now, listen, Julie——

JULIA. *(Sweetly, hoping he will)* Of course I'll
listen, Spike, if you want to apologize——

HOYT. *(Begins to do so)* Well, now, Julia, you
know I——

HUB. *(Mischievously)* Of course Julia will ac-
cept a public apology. (HOYT *starts to speak.)*

PROFESSOR. *(Innocently)* Of course—— (MAG-
PIE, HUB, JULIA, PROFESSOR, BETTY *and* PIERCE
crowd closer, embarrassing HOYT.)

MAGPIE. Better hurry up and make it, Hoyt—or
John will come in here and throw you out!

HOYT. *(Losing his temper)* Don't worry—I'm
not going to apologize. You can just stick to that
Jack the Ripper, Julia—but you mark my words—
some day he'll break out—and they'll find you all
cut up in a trunk! (ALL *laugh.* MAGPIE *goes up*
R.)

JULIA. And you're not going to apologize for
that last remark?

HOYT. *(Angrily)* No! I'm just going to go
back to Wisconsin and tell everybody that my girl
rooted for Ohio and sold me out for this four-eyed
murderer. So when you get back to school *you'd*
better be ready to do a little apologizing yourself.

JULIA. *(Furious)* Oh—had I? Well—I'll fool
you! *(Turns to* HUB) Hub, you live here in Columbus, don't you?

HUB. Yes——

JULIA. You come with me—I want you to help
me. *(Moves up C.)* And when I come back you'll

get a surprise, Mr. Hoyt. *(Exit* JULIA *and* HUB *up* L.*)*

(MUSIC Stops.)

HOYT. Where's she going?

MAGPIE. Don't worry. She's a nice girl. She's going to get John to sock you in the jaw.

PROFESSOR. Hush—here he comes . . .

(Music cue. Any jazz record. Once through till cue. MAGPIE—*"red card to hang out on the porch."* HOYT *starts* L. HUB *goes up, later joins* JULIA.*)*

MAGPIE. Don't run away, Hoyt.

HOYT. *(Turning angrily)* Who's running?

*(*JOHN *enters center, from* R.*, dressed in* MAGPIE'S *wide white trousers, tweed coat, foulard tie, and partially subdued cowlick. He still wears the glasses, but looks a great deal better.)*

MAGPIE. Here he is!

PROFESSOR. Hail, John . . .

MAGPIE. Doesn't he look wonderful, girls?

JOHN. *(Looking at pants)* They feel kind of wide.

REGGIE. *(Comes to* JOHN'S *left, with sandwiches)* Oh, there's the hero.

MAGPIE. Yes, step up, girls, and meet my pants.

JOHN. Oh, say—— *(*REGGIE *and* BETTY *dash up to him.)*

MAGPIE. This is Betty Fair and Regina Hopper, Your Majesty.

REGGIE. Oh, just call me Reggie. *(Shakes hands and smiles her best.)*

BETTY. *(On his* R. *Horning in)* Oh, I'm just dying to meet you. *(*REGGIE *gets sandwiches on plate* L. *and offers to* JOHN.*)*

REGGIE. *(To* HUB*)* Oh, when I think you won the race I could kiss you.

MAGPIE. Go ahead, don't mind me.

JOHN. *(Embarrassed)* Oh, say—— *(The* GIRLS *giggle.)*

BETTY. I will if you will, Reggie.

JOHN. Well—if you don't mind—I'd rather have a sandwich. *(He takes one in each hand.)* I'm very pleased to meet you . . . both of you—— *(Eats one sandwich in embarrassment, then other one.)*

BETTY. Isn't he cute! *(Pinches his cheek and he hands her the sandwich.* REGGIE *retires with sandwiches down* L.*)*

MAGPIE. Don't you want to kiss him, Hoyt? *(*JOHN *moves* R. *of* BETTY, *alarmed at* HOYT's *presence.)*

HOYT. Oh, shut up!

MAGPIE. Come on, John. Make a speech! *(*JOHN *shakes his head vigorously and indicates his mouth is full of sandwich. He swallows it.* JOHN *crosses* D. *and* R. *Stops short as he sees* MARGIE. MARGIE *enters from porch.)*

MARGIE. *(Stops as she sees him. Comes to him and takes his hand)* Oh, John——

JOHN. *(Choking)* Hello, Margie——

MARGIE. What is it?

JOHN. Peanut butter!

MARGIE. Everybody's proud of you, John; I'm so happy, and look, there's the Gold Cup.

JOHN. *(Picks it up, delighted)* Oh, look! It has my name on it. Well, what do you think of that!

HOYT. I'll tell you what I think of it—— *(*JULIA *entering with* HUB. HOYT *sees* JULIA *and turns away.)*

MAGPIE. Say, what have you two been up to?

JULIA. *(Very significantly)* We've been tele-

phoning. We've just been making some plans for Jack's future.

PIERCE. (*Up* L.) You mean in athletics?

JULIA. (*Center*) No—his real future—in business.

JOHN. (*Turning at piano*) In *business?*

JULIA. Yes, in business—I don't mind telling you all that I have a very good reason to be *interested* in John's future . . . (*She smiles proudly, and pauses.* HOYT *pointedly takes a chair, turns his back and sits down at other side of room. Nudges and whispers from the group.*)

PROFESSOR. (R.C.) Business? Why, John, I thought you were going to become a Professor.

HUB. (L.C.) Oh, but Mr. Deming, how much does that pay?

PROFESSOR. (*Smiling*) About twelve hundred a year . . .

JULIA. (L.C.) It's ridiculous to go to school for four years to learn how to make twelve hundred dollars.

PROFESSOR. (*Sensing that something is up*) Well, of course if you want to *make money*, John—— (*Turns upstage.* JOHN *looks from one to the other, bewildered.*)

MAGPIE. (L.C.) Sure—get into *business!* I can get you a job in my brother's firm, selling advertising.

JOHN. (*Center*, R. *of others*) But I don't know anything *about* advertising!

MAGPIE. That doesn't matter—neither does he. (JOHN *looks unhappy.*)

HUB. (*Crossing* MAGPIE *to* C.) Never mind— I've fixed it. I'm going to get him a job with father as a *bond salesman!*

MAGPIE. What?

HUB. (*Proudly*) A bond salesman!

JULIA. *(To* JOHN*)* Yes, that's more *unusual.* (HUB *nods proudly.)*

MARGIE. (R.) But do you think John would like it?

JULIA. *(Crosses* R.*)* He can *learn* to like it! It's nicer than fooling with cactuses.

JOHN. That reminds me—— *(Removes cactus from pocket.)*

JULIA. He's got it in his pocket. *(Crosses* L. *to end of sofa.)*

JOHN. I wanted to discuss it with you, Professor. (JOHN *turns to* PROFESSOR R.C.*)*

HUB. *(Interrupting)* And you couldn't go into a better field than selling bonds.

JOHN. You mean I would have to go around personally and sell them to people?

HUB. Sure!

JOHN. But how can you tell if they want any?

MAGPIE. Why, you give them a big red card—to hang out on the porch. *(Sits* R. *arm of sofa. Music stops.)*

JOHN. I wouldn't have time—I'm so busy working on my thesis in Botany.

JULIA. *(Forcefully)* You'll have to give up your thesis in botany—because you start selling bonds *Monday.*

JOHN. *(Wildly)* Monday?—why should I start Monday? What's the *hurry?*

JULIA. Well . . . that's my surprise . . . (HOYT *cannot conceal his real interest.)*

ALL. Oh!!!

JULIA. *(Enjoying the sensation)* Listen very carefully, Mr. Hoyt—— After the dance is over, at midnight, you're all invited to our *wedding!* *(Everybody gasps.)*

ALL. Your wedding!

MARGIE. *(Faintly)* Your wedding? Tonight?

JULIA. Yes. At midnight.

JOHN. *(Turns to her desperately as realization grows)* You don't mean this *coming* midnight?

JULIA. *(Takes his arm)* Yes, dear.

HOYT. *(Down L. Gulping)* You're going to marry him *tonight?*

JULIA. Yes, Mr. Hoyt—I can't hurry it any more —just to please you. (HOYT *snorts and turns away.)*

MARGIE. *(Faintly)* Didn't you know about it, John?

JOHN. *(Gulping)* No . . . *(The group responds with giggles, etc.)*

JULIA. He didn't know it was going to be so *soon* —that's the *surprise*—— Well, aren't you going to say something, Jack?

JOHN. *(Tries to laugh)* Ha, ha . . . yes—that was a surprise, all right!

HUB. *(Taking charge)* We've made all the arrangements, John—it's all fixed! The license, and the minister, and everything. I phoned and arranged it with the license clerk.

JULIA. He was *so* nice.

HUB. Yes . . . he owes me money.

JULIA. And he's going to meet us with the license at the minister's. *(She laughs; others join.* JOHN *tries to laugh.)*

JOHN. *(Weakly)* What minister?

JULIA. He lives right across the street. *(Indicates off* R.*)* He'll be ready at midnight.

JOHN. Oh, he won't want to stay up so late——

JULIA. It's all arranged. Now go and put on Magpie's dinner coat.

MAGPIE. Say, he's got my pants on now.

JULIA. And afterward Hub is going to drive us home!

JOHN. *(Weakly)* Home?

JULIA. To Jonesville to Pa—Pa's.

JOHN. Oh, they won't be expecting—— They might not have *room* for me.

JULIA. We can have *my* room, silly.

JOHN. Yes, but—— *Oh!* *(Realizes)* I'm used to so *much* room—I'm so *restless*—— *(Stops, terrified, as he gets in deeper.* JULIA *steps back down* R. *below piano.)*

HOYT. *(Steps forward furiously)* Say, who do you think you're kidding?

JOHN. *(C.)* What?

HOYT. *(Stepping up to* JOHN*)* So you didn't know anything about this wedding—it's all a surprise to you?

JOHN. Yes, it certainly is, Mr. Hoyt——

HOYT. Don't try to get friendly—you can't kid me.

PIERCE. *(L. of* HOYT. *To* HOYT *quietly)* Now, listen, Hoyt—calm down and behave yourself.

HOYT. *(Furiously)* I am calm! *(Turns back to* JOHN*)* But don't think you're fooling anybody with this innocent stuff!

JULIA. Oh, be still, Spike!

HOYT. I won't be still—for two cents I'd knock this bird for a goal! *(Glares at* JOHN*)* —crippled as I am! It wasn't enough for you to spike me so I can't walk—and to steal my girl from me—no, you had to frame up a *surprise* here in front of everybody—so you could all have the laugh on me!

MAGPIE, HUB *and* PIERCE. Listen, Hoyt—we didn't intend——

JOHN. *(Topping them)* Honest—I didn't mean to do anything like that—

HOYT. You're a liar! *(Glares at him, with chip on shoulder.)*

JOHN. *(Feeling he should do something about it)* Say—don't you call me a liar.

HOYT. You're a *liar*—what are you going to do about it?

JOHN. Why, I suppose I ought to do *something*— *(Removes glasses. Starts to remove coat, feeling that it is expected of him. Turns halfway from* HOYT. HOYT *reaches out and gives* JOHN *a push.)*

JULIA, BETTY *and* REGGIE. Oh—don't fight!

JOHN. *(As boys grab* HOYT*)* Hold him!

PIERCE. We have him.

JOHN. Have you got him?

BOYS. Yes!

JOHN. Thank you! *(Kicks* HOYT. HOYT *yells and in the excitement* JOHN *gets cactus from pocket and slaps it on* HOYT's *leg.)*

HOYT. *(Removing cactus)* Keep him away from me—I'm *murdered*——! *(*HUB *holds* JOHN.*)*

JOHN. Let me at him! *(Struggling.)*

MAGPIE. Don't kick him again!

JOHN. I don't want to kick him. I want my cactus back!

HOYT. *(Limping up stage)* Take the damn thing. *(Throws it down.)* Right where he spiked me—— I *told* you, Julia—— He's a murderer! *(Up to door center.)*

JULIA. *(Crossing behind piano)* It was your own fault—— Oh, Spike—aren't you going to stay for the wedding?

HOYT. *(Giving her a look of pitiful rage)* Oh— you just want to break my heart—you damned oil-can! *(He limps off center, boiling with indignation. All crowd around* JOHN, *congratulating and patting him on the back, etc.)*

MAGPIE. Johnny, you're a fighting fool!

JULIA. And he did it all for me!

HUB. He fought for his woman and won her!

MAGPIE. The *worm* has *turned*! *(Slaps* JOHN *on back.)*

JOHN. *(Brandishing cactus)* Did you say I was a worm?

MAGPIE. No! *(Crosses left.)*

PROFESSOR. *(Down* R. *Hastily)* He meant it as a compliment, John.

JULIA. Now go and get ready, Jack.

JOHN. *(Crossing to her center)* Say, listen—I can't get married so suddenly like this——

JULIA. Yes, you can, Jack. Now don't be bashful —we want to be congratulated——

BETTY *and* REGGIE. *(Rushing up excitedly)* We want to celebrate. We want to tell the others! *(Exit center.)*

(Music cue. Victor record No. 19433a., *repeat till cue—*MARGIE, *"You'll have to do that alone.")*

MAGPIE. *(Up* C.*)* You settled who's going to marry Julia—*you* are!

(MUSIC Starts.)

JULIA. *(Radiantly)* And you can thank Spike Hoyt for this, Jack! (JULIA *exits with* MAGPIE.*)*

HUB. *(Who has been pounding* JOHN *on the back, wheels him around. Crosses* R.*)* You can put on that Tuxedo yourself. We've only got about ten minutes. I must get my car ready. *(Rushes out down* R. *All these lines are fast and excited up to* HUB's *exit.)*

JOHN. *(Dazed by the rush)* Must you? *(Turns up; finds* JULIA *gone)* Hey—listen! *(Turns back to* PROFESSOR; *speaks with belated desperation)* Say —this is *serious!* (Moves down center) Prof, can I speak to you a minute alone about—something?

PROFESSOR. *(At piano with* MARGIE*)* You haven't time, John—you must put on Magpie's tuxedo. *(Crosses to* R.C.*)*

JOHN. *(Turns center)* I'm not going to. These pants are bad enough.

PROFESSOR. You must learn to be careful about your clothes now, John. Your wife will insist on it.

JOHN. *(Dazed)* Who?

PROFESSOR. Your wife.

JOHN. *(Pretty well sunk)* Oh . . . yes. *(Crosses* L.C.*)*

PROFESSOR. *(Burning it in)* And you must be down bright and early to the office every morning— to get that nice long list of people to sell bonds to— I did have a couple of new specimens of confervae I wanted to show you Monday—but I suppose you won't have much time for that now, eh?

JOHN. Oh—I'd love to see them!

PROFESSOR. But Julia is putting you to work Monday.

JOHN. Oh . . . yes . . .

PROFESSOR. *(Aside to* MARGIE*)* Margie, *"precipitate"!*

MARGIE. *(Moving to* R.C. *Quickly)* Are confervae like Algae?

JOHN. *(Crossing to her. Eagerly)* Yes, fresh- water plants—I hate to abandon my Algae, Pro- fessor.

PROFESSOR. *(Up* C. *Brusquely)* Oh, you must forget all that—it takes a great deal of courage to be interested in Algae nowadays, John—it's much better for you to be a bond salesman.

*(*FRESHMAN *enters from up left; comes down* L.C.*)*

FRESHMAN. Margie, may I have this dance?

MARGIE. *(Right)* Well, I . . .

JOHN. *(*R.C. *Bravely)* She and I are going to sit it out.

PROFESSOR. *(Exchanges a look with* MARGIE. FRESHMAN *has not budged)* You can take me along, Norton. A male chaperon must work at his job. *(Pushes* FRESHMAN *out, and follows.)*

FRESHMAN. *(Moving out)* All right, sir. But I—— *(Exit* FRESHMAN *and* PROFESSOR.*)*

JOHN. I wish he had stayed here. I wanted to talk to him.

MARGIE. What about?

JOHN. Listen, you may as well know the truth about me, Margie—I'm no good. *(Crosses L.; sits on sofa.)*

MARGIE. Oh, yes, you are. Why, just look at what you've done today.

JOHN. I don't mean that. I mean *morally* . . . Here I've got a chance to be everything I ever hoped for—and I don't *appreciate* it. I don't seem to *want* to be any good. Now, I know there's no money in being a professor, for instance, but I don't care! Now see—that isn't even *patriotic!* It's just *ridiculous*.

MARGIE. I don't think so. Most of the really great scientists have been like that, John.

JOHN. Oh, but it isn't only about Botany—that isn't the worst of it. *(Crosses R.C.)*

MARGIE. *(Hopefully)* Oh, is there something else?

JOHN. *(Slowly, looking away from her)* Yes. I'm just beginning to realize it . . . I know you'll despise me, but . . . well . . . that feeling I got this afternoon wasn't *right,* either.

MARGIE. What feeling?

JOHN. *(Turning to her)* In the tent—when you . . . remember I told you I felt as if I was on wings or something?

MARGIE. *(Nodding that she remembers)* Why wasn't it right?

JOHN. *(Looks front. Happily)* Because . . . I got it again tonight.

MARGIE. When Julia told you about the wedding?

JOHN. *(Face falls)* No, I *lost* it then.

MARGIE. *(Softly)* When did you get it, John?

JOHN. *(Softly and sincerely)* When you came in and spoke to me.

MARGIE. When?

JOHN. *(Very sincerely)* Just when I was eating that sandwich. I had my mouth all full of peanut butter, but that feeling came over me *just the same*.

MARGIE. Oh, John——

JOHN. *(In despair)* It seems things always happen to me when I'm eating—just like that noodle soup.

MARGIE. Oh, John—you dear, *simple*——

JOHN. *(Hopelessly)* I *knew* you would despise me.

MARGIE. *(Tenderly)* I don't despise you, John. You're a dear boy—and I'm going to tell Julia she has no right to——

JOHN. *(Despairingly)* Oh, she knows what's best for me . . . she's analyzed me. I found out what some of the things mean that are wrong with me, and it was even worse than I thought. No . . . I've got to go through with it. I sort of agreed to it—here in front of everybody.

MARGIE. *(Center. Sadly)* Then we must say good-bye now.

JOHN. *(Nodding, with difficulty. Takes pin from lapel)* I . . . I realize that *you* just . . . *did that* this *afternoon* to help me, for her sake—but would you let me give you something—to keep? *(She nods. He silently holds out his pledge pin.)*

MARGIE. *(Touched)* Why, John, it's your pledge pin. Your Psi Sigma pledge pin!

JOHN. *(Trying to restrain his emotion)* Huh huh. I won't need it now—just put it away, in an old box or something . . . I'd rather *you'd* have it.

MARGIE. That pin is dearer to you than anything in the world, isn't it?

JOHN. Oh, yes . . . in a way . . .

MARGIE. And you're giving it to me?

JOHN. Do you mind?

MARGIE. *(Takes pin; keeps his hand)* I'll keep it . . . always. *(She holds his hand against her face, kisses it quickly and lets it go. Starts up* C.*)*
(MUSIC Stops.)

JOHN. *(Stands dazed, holding hand as she left it; speaks suddenly)* Wait! *I'm gonna* POSTPONE *that wedding!*

MARGIE. *(Startled)* No, you can't do that, John.

JOHN. *(In great emotional excitement)* Yes, I can. Until the first of the week, anyhow—my mother will be here then and she can tell me what to do. *(Moves* R.*)* That minister is right across the street—I'll go over and tell him to go to hell——Go to bed. You come with me!

MARGIE. *(Holding his arm)* No, John. There's no good in postponing it. You've got to make up your mind now to be one kind of person or the other. It will be easier for you to be Julia's kind—you'll have her to help you.

JOHN. Why do I have to amount to anything if I don't want to? Can't I just be myself?

MARGIE. *(Eagerly)* *Yes*—but nobody can help you decide, John. You'll have to do that alone.

(JULIA enters with SPIKE. HUB, PROFESSOR, MAGPIE and others follow.)

JULIA. *(*L.C. *with* SPIKE. HUB L. *of* JULIA*)* Where have you two been?

MARGIE. *(*L. *of* JOHN*)* Why, we—that is, he—er——

JOHN. *(*R.C. *at end of piano)* Well, where have *you* two been?

JULIA. Why, we—that is, he—Spike and I were just dancing—— We were waiting for *you*.

HOYT. *(Steps forward, remembering his limp)* I'll tell him, Julia . . .

JOHN. *(Desperately. Steps center)* No, you won't! From now on nobody is going to tell me anything!

MAGPIE. (L. *end of sofa*) What?

JOHN. *(Removing coat. Tosses it)* Here's your coat, Hub——

HOYT. *(Edging away)* Now wait—— Don't let him start on me again——

JOHN. *(Fiercely)* Shut up! Magpie, I'll give you the pants later. (MAGPIE *is* D.L. *Turns to* HUB) And I won't need you to drive me to Zanesville tonight, Hub——

HUB. *(Down* LC., *below sofa)* All right—but what's the idea?

JOHN. And I won't be there to work Monday, either—I'm not going to dress up, or slick down my hair . . . or *sell bonds*.

PROFESSOR. *(Appearing up center)* What's the matter, John?

JULIA. (L.C.) Yes, for Heaven's sake . . . !

JOHN. You are all trying to make me *amount to something*, like you do—— Well, I can't—I'm inferior—and doggone it, I'm gonna *be* inferior. I'm going to be a professor, whether it's immoral or not. *(Turns to* MARGIE, *turns back, faces* JULIA) And what's more, I'm going to be a *darned good* professor.

HUB. But you can't, old man. Julia won't stand for it!

(WARN Curtain.)

JOHN. Julia has nothing to do with it.

HOYT. She hasn't—— Why, I thought——

MAGPIE. But she's going to marry you!

JOHN. *(With desperate idea)* I'd like to see her try it—she'd be a bigamist.

HUB *and* JULIA. What?

JOHN. I am married!

ALL OF THEM. What? What's that? etc.

MARGIE. What?

JOHN. *(Wildly)* Yes, to her. *(Nudges MARGIE)* *Aren't we?*

MARGIE. Huh?

JULIA. To you?

MARGIE. *(As JOHN nudges her again)* Yes, . . . to me . . . He just made me do it . . .

JULIA. I don't believe it. It isn't true.

JOHN. *(After an instant)* Well, she's my wife in the sight of Heaven, anyway!

JULIA. What!

JOHN. Yes—it *happened this afternoon—in the tent!*

(All gasp and exclaim. JOHN is suddenly horrified as he realizes what they think.)

JULIA. *What did?*

MARGIE. I kissed him! *(General relief.)*

JOHN. Well—I didn't *resist* her!

PROFESSOR. *(Slaps JOHN on back)* Dear, dear— this is *terrible!*

JOHN. I know it, but that's the way *I am!* I'm an *immoral introvert!*

JULIA. You're a *what?*

JOHN. Oh, I found out what those words mean— you were trying to bring out my evil nature! Well, you did, all right—— Come on, Margie, now we *will* get married!

MARGIE. Oh, we can't get married like this!

JULIA. I should hope not!

HUB *and* MAGPIE. No.

JOHN. *(Shouting)* *Why* can't we? *Shut up,* all of you!—There's nothing too bad for me to do now! I can *get married* or anything! *(Turns to JULIA defiantly)* My *libido* is turned *outward!* *(Exits* D.R. *with MARGIE, walking in heroic strides, as the*

CURTAIN FALLS

IMPORTANT

(Note for Director)

The dialogue during the race scene, Act II, Scene II, which is typed with marginal stage directions for the crowds cheering, is really ad lib. and is only put into the script for individual direction. Few, if any, of these lines can possibly be heard above the cheering.

From the beginning of the race the cheer leader directs the scene and all follow his eyes and his mood. He gives the crowd several definite cues in pantomime as the race proceeds.

These are as follows :—

1. Page 80, Act II: Magpie changes from a triumphant war dance he has been doing along the apron to a tragic turn upstage as Wisconsin gains the lead. He puts his hands to his head, and the crowd reacts, showing disappointment.

2. Page 81, Act II: As the third Ohio State runner reaches a point almost directly out front, Magpie leaps into the air as he sees his Ohio runner take the lead. The crowd comes to its feet with renewed cheers.

3. Page 82, Act II. This cue for the crowd comes when John drops the baton. They all join in lamentations, which gradually change into interest, then hope, as John gains.

4. Page 83, Act II. As John reaches direct front and catches up to Hoyt, Magpie again leaps in the air, followed by a great leap from Pierce. The

crowd now goes mad until end of race.   The crowd
dies down at end of race until the Announcement.

5. Cue for cheering, which continues until Julia
comes to John and Magpie holds up his hands.

6. Cue for hush, so that we hear the tag lines
clearly.   Then:—

7. Final loud cheer for Curtain.

These seven cues are all that you need to direct
the race scene.   The actors need only know the sense
of the lines through this part.

PROPS

ACT I

5 Bookcases with prop books (dummies).
2 Counters—1 long and 1 short. *2 small pads on counter.
1 Bookcase and display stand (combined).
1 Cash register and money.
2 Stools.
* 1 Counter file (spike).
1 Prop basket.
1 Pail (used in first and last act) and * 1 duster.
45 Books.
* 6 Leather note books.
* 2 Cactus.
* 1 Small bunch of wild flowers.
1 Glass case with pencils.
10 Stands—fountain pens—dummies.
   Also writing pads, note books, display cards.
1 Drawing set in case.
1 Mucilage stand (3 pieces).
1 Ground cloth (brown).
1 Pipe and tobacco.
1 Comb.
1 Small mirror.
1 Postal card stand.
1 Step ladder in window.

OFF STAGE

* 18 Books (in pile), foot of stepladder in cellar.
* 12 Books (2 piles, 6 each), at door up-stage L.C.
1 Resin box at door L.C.

   * *Hand Props.*

111

* 6 Leather note books.
1 Apple.
* 1 Bunch wild flowers.
* 2 Cactus.

ACT II

SCENE I

1 Table 8ft. x 2ft.6in.
6 Towels.
2 Gray blankets.
1 Strip ground cloth to cover white line.
2 Camp stools.
1 Basin.
1 Pail.
1 Quart bottle of water.
1 Pitcher of water.
1 Sloan's liniment bottle (half full).
1 Drinking cup.
1 Ground cloth.
1 Sponge.
1 Small table 2ft. x 2ft.

SCENE II

4 Small pieces of grass matting.
5 Large pieces of grass matting.
2 Sixteen-foot benches.
8 Small benches.
10 Pennants with poles.
* 1 Large megaphone.
* 1 Small megaphone.
* 2 Batons.
* 1 Revolver.
* 1 Tape for finish of race.

* Hand Props.

1 Carpet for padding under ground cloth.
6 Strips red bunting.
6 Strips gray bunting.
* 2 Ohio blankets.
1 Coin.

OFF-STAGE

* 2 Batons.
* 1 Small megaphone.
* 1 Small note book.
* 1 Revolver.
* 1 Coin.
1 Gramaphone and records.

ACT III

2 Wall banners—1 Ohio and 1 Wisconsin.
3 Wall placques.
1 Piano—1 bench and music (baby grand).
1 Bookcase.
3 Couches.
1 Rug 10 x 18.
2 Tables—1 library and 1 consul.
2 Library chairs.
1 Armchair.
2 Candlesticks on mantel (brass).
3 Loving cups.
5 Loving cups on bookcase.
1 Cover for library table.
1 Cover for consul table.
1 Piano throw.
1 Punch bowl with base, dipper and 8 cups (with
     grapejuice).
4 Plates on library table with prop sandwiches.
1 Prop cake on stand.
4 Peanut butter sandwiches.

Hands Props.

1 Lace curtain on door L.
2 Blue portierres.
1 Brass rod.
2 Book ends, 7 Books, on table back of couch.
2 Magazines.
1 Set of fire dogs.
1 Prop basket.
1 Picture.
1 Mantel.
* 2 Cactus.
2 Sofa cushions.

OFF-STAGE

* 1 Gold cup at door D.R.
1 Gramaphone and records L.
* 1 Flask.

SPECIAL

18 Special books in cellar—Act I.
Grapejuice for punch bowl.
4 Peanut butter sandwiches.
5 Books on counter—Act I.
1 Psycho-analysis book—Act I.
Bon Ami for window—Act I.

LIGHTING PLOT

ACT I

Foots. Amber and white ⅞.
All X-ray border.
All spots.
Strip over door L.C., 7 amber.
Strip side of door R., 2 white.

Hand props.

Baby spot amber through cut in window (see dia-
    gram).
Spot on window.

ACT II.   SCENE I

Foots.   White and amber.   Full.
Strip and 3 baby spots in tint.
6—1000 watts Amber overhead tent.
4—1000 watts White overhead tent.
1—1000 watts in entrance.

ACT II.   SCENE II

Foots.   White and amber.
All X-ray border.
All Spots.
All 1000 watts.   6 amber, 3 blue, 4 white.

ACT III

Foots.   Amber, Pink and White.   Full.
Chandelier and 2 wall brackets.
Piano lamp and table lamp.
All X-ray border.
All Spots.

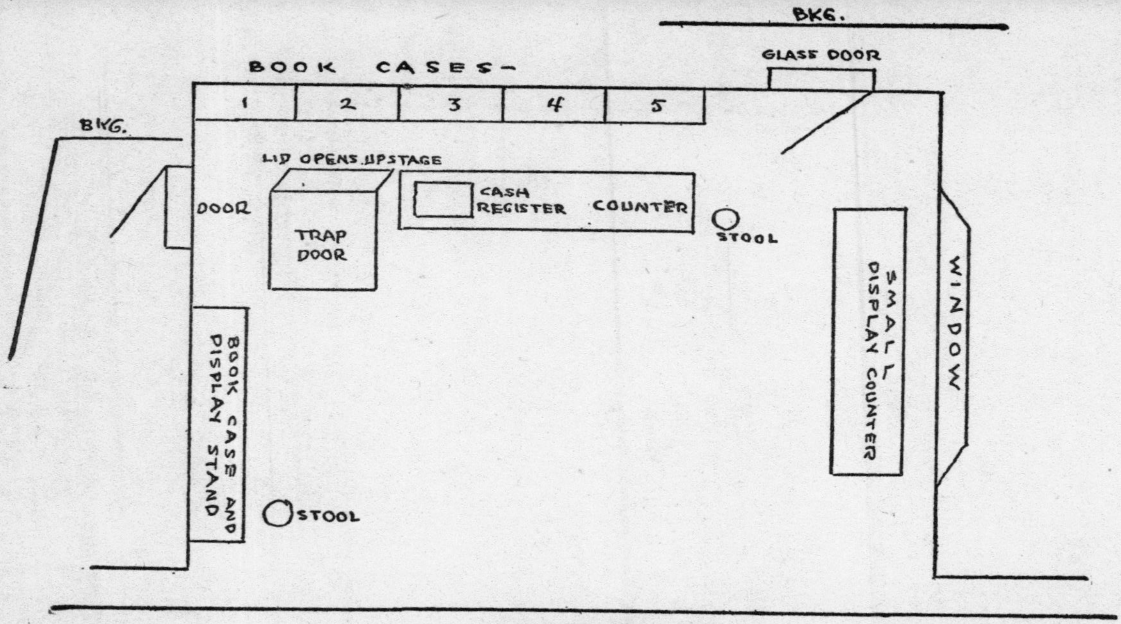

SCENE DESIGN

THE POOR NUT

ACT I

BOOK CASES —

1 2 3 4 5

BOOK CASE AND DISPLAY STAND

DOOR

LID OPENS UPSTAGE

TRAP DOOR

CASH REGISTER COUNTER

STOOL

STOOL

GLASS DOOR

SMALL DISPLAY COUNTER

WINDOW

BKG.

BKG.

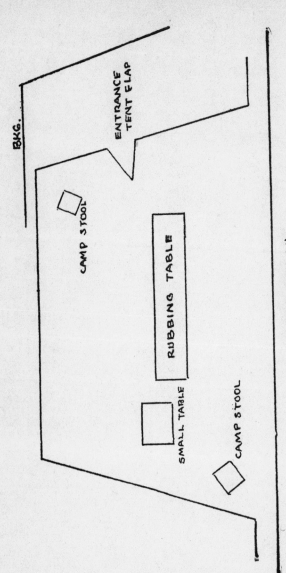

BKG.

ENTRANCE
TENT FLAP

CAMP STOOL

RUBBING TABLE

SMALL TABLE

CAMP STOOL

SCENE DESIGN
THE POOR NUT
ACT I SCENE I.

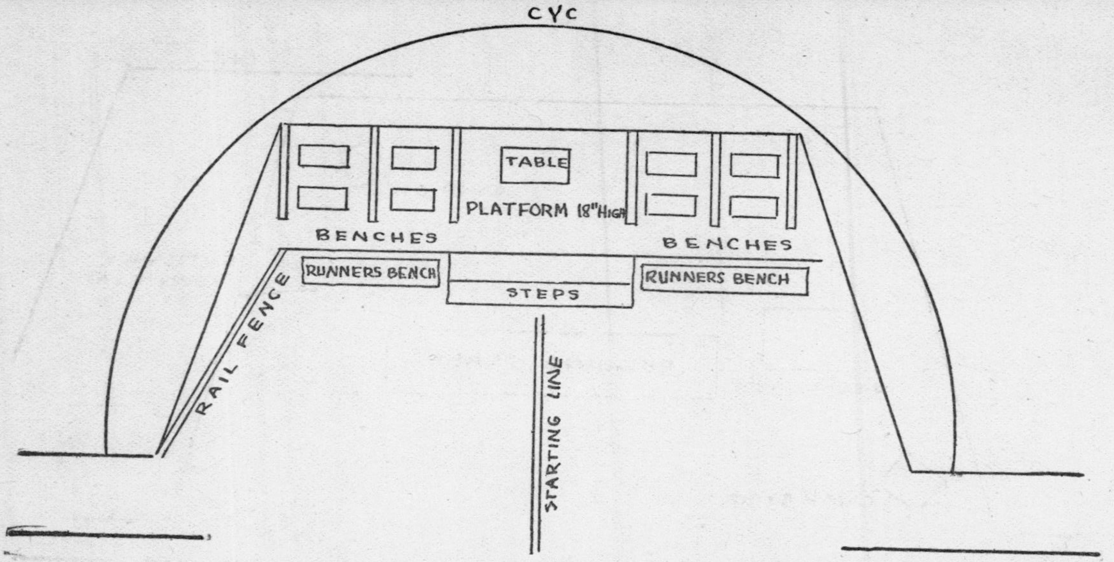

RAIL FENCE

RUNNERS BENCH

BENCHES

PLATFORM 18" High

TABLE

STEPS

STARTING LINE

RUNNERS BENCH

BENCHES

CYC

SCENE DESIGN
THE POOR NUT
ACT II SCENE 2

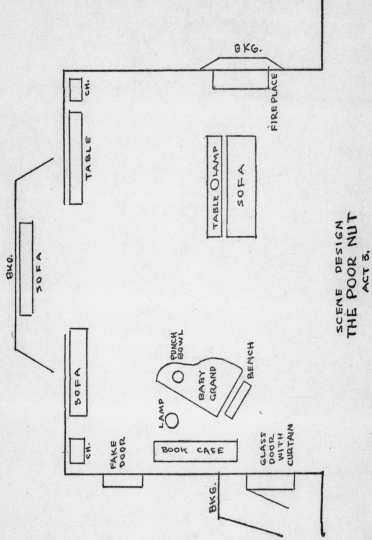

SCENE DESIGN
THE POOR NUT
ACT 3.

POLLYANNA

"The glad play," in 3 acts. By Catherine Chisholm Cushing. Based on the novel by Eleanor H. Porter. 5 males, 6 females. 2 interiors. Costumes, modern. Plays 2¼ hours.

The story has to do with the experiences of an orphan girl who is thrust, unwelcome, into the home of a maiden aunt. In spite of the tribulations that beset her life she manages to find something to be glad about, and brings light into sunless lives. Finally, Pollyanna straightens out the love affairs of her elders, and last, but not least, finds happiness for herself in the heart of Jimmy. "Pollyanna" is a glad play and one which is bound to give one a better appreciation of people and the world. It reflects the humor, tenderness and humanity that gave the story such wonderful popularity among young and old.

Produced at the Hudson Theatre, New York, and for two seasons on tour, by George C. Tyler, with Helen Hayes in the part of "Pollyanna." (Royalty, twenty-five dollars.) Price, 75 Cents.

THE CHARM SCHOOL

A comedy in 3 acts. By Alice Duer Miller and Robert Milton. 6 males, 10 females (may be played by 5 males and 8 females). Any number of school girls may be used in the ensembles. Scenes, 2 interiors. Modern costumes. Plays 2½ hours.

The story of "The Charm School" is familiar to Mrs. Miller's readers. It relates the adventures of a handsome young automobile salesman, scarcely out of his 'teens, who, upon inheriting a girls' boarding-school from a maiden aunt, insists on running it himself, according to his own ideas, chief of which is, by the way, that the dominant feature in the education of the young girls of to-day should be CHARM. The situations that arise are teeming with humor—clean, wholesome humor. In the end the young man gives up the school, and promises to wait until the most precocious of his pupils reaches a marriageable age. The play has the freshness of youth, the inspiration of an extravagant but novel idea, the charm of originality, and the promise of wholesome, sanely amusing, pleasant entertainment. We strongly recommend it for high school production. It was first produced at the Bijou Theatre, New York, then toured the country. Two companies are now playing it in England. (Royalty, twenty-five dollars.)
Price, 75 Cents.

SAMUEL FRENCH, 25 West 45th Street, New York City
Our new descriptive catalogue sent free on request.

ON THE HIRING LINE

Comedy in 3 acts, by Harvey O'Higgins and Harriet Ford. 5 males, 4 females. Interior throughout. Costumes, modern. Plays 2½ hours.

Sherman Fessenden, unable to induce servants to remain for any reasonable length of time at his home, hits upon the novel expedient of engaging detectives to serve as domestics.

His second wife, an actress, weary of the country and longing for Broadway, has succeeded in discouraging every other cook and butler against remaining long at the house, believing that by so doing she will win her husband to her theory that country life is dead. So she is deeply disappointed when she finds she cannot discourage the new servants.

The sleuths, believing they had been called to report on the actions of those living with the Fessendens, proceeded to warn Mr. Fessenden that his wife has been receiving love-notes from Steve Mark, an actor friend, and that his daughter has been planning to elope with a thief.

One sleuth causes an uproar in the house, making a mess of the situations he has witnessed. Mr. Fessenden, however, has learned a lesson and is quite willing to leave the servant problem to his wife thereafter. (Royalty, twenty-five dollars.)

Price, 75 Cents.

A FULL HOUSE

A farcical comedy in 3 acts. By Fred Jackson. 7 males, 7 females. One interior scene. Modern costumes. Time, 2½ hours.

Imagine a reckless and wealthy youth who writes ardent love letters to a designing chorus girl, an attorney brother-in-law who steals the letters and then gets his hand-bag mixed up with the grip of a burglar who has just stolen a valuable necklace from the mother of the indiscreet youth, and the efforts of the crook to recover his plunder, as incidents in the story of a play in which the swiftness of the action never halts for an instant. Not only are the situations screamingly funny but the lines themselves hold a fund of humor at all times. This newest and cleverest of all farces was written by Fred Jackson, the well-known short-story writer, and is backed up by the prestige of an impressive New York success and the promise of unlimited fun presented in the most attractive form. A cleaner, cleverer farce has not been seen for many a long day. "A Full House" is a house full of laughs. (Royalty, twenty-five dollars.)

Price, 75 Cents.

SAMUEL FRENCH, 25 West 45th Street, New York City
Our new descriptive catalogue sent free on request

TWEEDLES

Comedy in 3 acts, by Booth Tarkington and Harry Leon Wilson. 5 males, 4 females. 1 interior. Costumes, modern. Plays 2½ hours.

Julian, scion of the blue-blooded Castleburys, falls in love with Winsora Tweedle, daughter of the oldest family in a Maine village. The Tweedles esteem the name because it has been rooted in the community for 200 years, and they look down on "summer people" with the vigor that only "summer boarder" communities know.

The Castleburys are aghast at the possibility of a match, and call on the Tweedles to urge how impossible such an alliance would be. Mr. Castlebury laboriously explains the barrier of social caste, and the elder Tweedle takes it that these unimportant summer folk are terrified at the social eminence of the Tweedles.

Tweedle generously agrees to co-operate with the Castleburys to prevent the match. But Winsora brings her father to realize that in reality the Castleburys look upon them as inferiors. The old man is infuriated, and threatens vengeance, but is checkmated when Julian unearths a number of family skeletons and argues that father isn't a Tweedle, since the blood has been so diluted that little remains. Also, Winsora takes the matter into her own hands and outfaces the old man. So the youngsters go forth triumphant. "Tweedles" is Booth Tarkington at his best. (Royalty, twenty-five dollars.)   Price, 75 Cents.

JUST SUPPOSE

A whimsical comedy in 3 acts, by A. E. Thomas, author of "Her Husband's Wife," "Come Out of the Kitchen," etc. 6 males, 2 females. 1 interior, 1 exterior. Costumes, modern. Plays 2¼ hours.

It was rumored that during his last visit the Prince of Wales appeared for a brief spell under an assumed name somewhere in Virginia. It is on this story that A. E. Thomas based "Just Suppose." The theme is handled in an original manner. Linda Lee Stafford meets one George Shipley (in reality is the Prince of Wales). It is a case of love at first sight, but, alas, princes cannot select their mates and thereby hangs a tale which Mr. Thomas has woven with infinite charm. The atmosphere of the South with its chivalry dominates the story, touching in its sentiment and lightened here and there with delightful comedy. "Just Suppose" scored a big hit at the Henry Miller Theatre New York, with Patricia Collinge. (Royalty, twenty-five dollars.)   Price, 75 Cents.